NEVER AGAIN

NEVER AGAIN

A Never Before Told
Insight Into
The 1992 Los Angeles Riots

BILL C. WEISS

New York

NEVER AGAIN
A Never Before Told Insight Into The 1992 Los Angeles Riots

Published in New York, New York, by Morgan James Publishing. Morgan James and The Entrepreneurial Publisher are trademarks of Morgan James, LLC. www.MorganJamesPublishing.com

The Morgan James Speakers Group can bring authors to your live event. For more information or to book an event visit The Morgan James Speakers Group at www.TheMorganJamesSpeakersGroup.com.

DISCLAIMER: Names have been changed to safeguard the reputations of those involved. Transcripts have been made from actual radio and TV news footage.

Shelfie

A free eBook edition is available with the purchase of this print book.

CLEARLY PRINT YOUR NAME ABOVE IN UPPER CASE

Instructions to claim your free eBook edition:
1. Download the Shelfie app for Android or iOS
2. Write your name in **UPPER CASE** above
3. Use the Shelfie app to submit a photo
4. Download your eBook to any device

ISBN 978-1-63047-904-6 paperback
ISBN 978-1-63047-905-3 eBook
ISBN 978-1-63047-906-0 hardcover
Library of Congress Control Number:
2015920169

Cover Design by:
John Weber

In an effort to support local communities and raise awareness and funds, Morgan James Publishing donates a percentage of all book sales for the life of each book to Habitat for Humanity Peninsula and Greater Williamsburg.

Get involved today, visit
www.MorganJamesBuilds.com

Habitat
for Humanity®
Peninsula and
Greater Williamsburg
Building Partner

DEDICATION

In memory of those who lost their lives or were severely injured in the civil disturbance of April 29-May 3, 1992, in Los Angeles, California.

TABLE OF CONTENTS

ACKNOWLEDGMENTS

It is not without discipline and hard work that a book can be published. I would like to thank my book coach, Judith Cassis for her knowledge, guidance, wisdom, and constant support to make this project possible. Her critique, insight, feedback, and editing was invaluable.

I must also thank Mar Preston, who so dearly assisted in the proofreading, and provided supplemental editing and developmental ideas to the project.

I would like to thank Bill Blowers, himself a fairly new author at the time, for his suggestions, clarifications, and assistance while helping me with several issues during the various stages of this journey.

With regard to Morgan James Publishing, none of this would have been possible without getting the first break at Author 101 University when Jim Howard gave my story a chance and directed me to Terry Whalin. Terry was extremely informative and helped direct my project through the review process. I also sincerely appreciate the support, communications, and guidance from my managing editor, Megan Malone.

DISCLAIMER

Some names have been changed to safeguard the reputations of those involved. Transcripts have been taken from actual radio and TV news footage.

INTRODUCTION

Gang violence and civil unrest contributed to 1992 being the deadliest year in Los Angeles County history. The number of people slain in Los Angeles (2,589) was up eight percent from the previous year. According to the *New York Times*, the carnage could have filled the downtown Los Angeles Ahmanson Theatre to more than capacity.

There were 517 murders in July and August alone. Although crime rates were high, that same year a scientific development occurred that directly impacted not only criminology, but the entire world. Connecting criminals with their crimes was refined as Geneticist Alec Jeffreys used DNA profiling methods developed in 1984. The new method allowed him to confirm the identity of the Nazi Doctor, Josef Mengele, comparing DNA obtained from a femur bone of his exhumed skeleton against DNA from his widow and son. The new technology upgraded the ability to confirm identities of suspects in future years, as well as vindicate some who were wrongly accused.

The year 1992 would not soon be forgotten. Pop culture idol Michael Jackson's number one hit, "Black or White" exploded on the charts. At the end of the music video Jackson is seen smashing windows, destroying a car, and detonating an explosion. The violence, mingled with Jackson's controversial and sexually explicit dance moves, prompted MTV and other music video networks to remove the last four minutes of the video prior to airing.

To make the violence more palpable to viewers, an altered version was produced, adding racist graffiti to the windows Jackson breaks. Nevertheless, MTV branded the video "one of the most controversial videos of all time" and it is still censored throughout the world.

Interestingly, a few months later, a similar scenario played out in real life as the worst civil disturbance in the United States in the 20th century erupted. One big difference: the violence was not censored. Looting, beatings and arson were broadcast across the world via live television in the style of *breathless Breaking News* reporting.

The spectacle began with an incident that occurred a year earlier. Stopped after a high speed pursuit, Rodney King resisted police orders and was struck over 50 times with a night stick. Witness George Holliday recorded the incident on video that was played on local TV station KTLA and eventually on networks worldwide. Both men became instant celebrities.

Holliday awoke at 12:45 AM to the sound of helicopters and sirens. He'd set his alarm clock to rise early so he could film a co-worker at the plumbing company he worked for who was training for the LA marathon.

Hearing the commotion on the street below, he peered out of his window and saw a man surrounded by police officers. Holliday dressed quickly and grabbed his camcorder to record the event. By the time he stepped out onto his balcony, King's beating had commenced. Several other residents filmed the event, but Holliday had the best vantage point. He was on the second floor of the apartment building. That video would be seen around the world, replayed countless times.

∾

On April 29, 1992, the acquittals of the four Los Angeles Police Department officers involved in the King beating left the City of Los Angeles stunned. African-Americans were enraged at what they perceived as gross injustice and took to the streets and the airwaves. Angry and violent crowds gathered on street corners across the city, while thousands more turned to their televisions to watch the news events unfold.

Spreading unchecked from the major flash point of the South Los Angeles intersection of Florence and Normandie Avenues, this chaotic disturbance engulfed the city and portions of the surrounding metropolitan area. Its effects would ripple across the nation and be observed throughout the world. Scars are still visible today.

The cost left in the wake of the riots extended far beyond that of mere financial loss. Mental and emotional affects, both during and after the riots, were substantial. Fear was rampant and progress made against racism in the decades prior was all but overturned as black and white, rich versus poor, went head to head.

∽

Other than the actual beating, trial, and verdicts, there were several underlying motives for the 1992 Los Angeles riots, also known as the Rodney King riots. In 1991 people were enraged over the acquittal of a Korean-American shop owner, Soon Ja Du, for the fatal shooting in the back of the head of a black teenager.

On March 16, 1991, 15-year-old Latisha Harlins walked into a neighborhood convenience store. Seeing her with a bottle of orange juice, store owner Soon Ja Du accused her of planning to steal the juice. She denied it. After harsh words and a physical confrontation, the shop owner shot the teen. She lay dying, clutching two dollars to pay for the orange juice. A videotape played during the trial also showed that Latasha Harlins had actually turned away from the scuffle with the Korean grocer when Son Ja Du shot the teenager in the back of the head.

Soon Ja Du was found guilty of voluntary manslaughter, but was sentenced to probation, community service, and fined $500. A dispute over a bottle of orange juice not only cost a life, but amped up the rampant racial tension between African-Americans and Korean-Americans.

Relations between blacks and Korean-Americans in the area had been rocky for some time. Frustration mounted as perceptions amongst blacks that Korean-American merchants were taking money out of their community while refusing to hire blacks. High rates of unemployment and growing economic disparity in Los Angeles also played a part. Inner city poverty, segregation, lack of educational and employment opportunities, seethed in combination with police abuse and mistrust. Poor police-community relations contributed as well to a volatile situation.

The number of people living below the official government poverty level in the U.S. was 36.9 million in 1992. This was 1.2 million higher than in 1991, and there was no sign of relief.

Mistrust of the police increased with the implementation of Operation Hammer or Big Blue Hammer, the origin of which can be traced back to the 1984 Olympics held in Los Angeles. Under the supervision of Chief Daryl Gates, the LAPD conducted massive gang sweeps resulting in numerous arrests; yet, there were few actual charges. The gang sweeps created a further wedge between the LAPD and the community that would take years to undo.

The operation was characterized by massive arrests. As many as a thousand youth were arrested at a time. The division between law enforcement and the community widened as the community witnessed the public humiliation and police-administered beatings. It is difficult to determine how widespread these events were as many went unreported. No apparent accountability for years of brutality, mostly by the LAPD, created a seething tension.

Starting in April of 1988, dozens of police officers, going neighborhood to neighborhood, arrested suspected gang members and drug dealers. Often times, those arrested were young teens who just happened to be in the wrong place at the wrong time.

In August of 1988 a band of 80 police officers acting on a tip raided and vandalized four apartment buildings. The tip had been inaccurate. Four officers were prosecuted on charges of felony vandalism. All were acquitted.

A historical examination of the strained relations between LAPD and African-American civilians is proof that it was not just the reading of the Rodney King verdict that ignited the flames of the riots. The verdict, broadcast over live TV was the immediate trigger, but many underlying factors provided the fuel for events to explode.

A long-standing perception that the LAPD engaged in racial profiling and used excessive force added to the community's frustration. Extremely high unemployment among residents of South Central Los Angeles, which had been hit very hard by the nationwide recession, also had people sitting on edge. As mentioned earlier, the crime rate continued to rise. In comparison, it was about four-times greater than it is today.

Additionally, a poor relationship and lack of communication existed between Mayor Tom Bradley and Police Chief Gates. Gates also had plans to retire in June of that year. Los Angeles was living through the deadliest period in its history. Gang activity was out of control, with homicides skyrocketing past the 2,000 mark countywide in 1991, and headed still higher in the first quarter of 1992. Nearly 40 percent of the killings were classified as gang related. The Rodney King verdicts were delivered in this hostile climate.

～

LAPD's slow response to the festering uprising allowed the disturbance to spread citywide as it went unchecked without immediate action. Poor command decisions and a lack of real planning by LAPD, coupled with several members of the command staff being out of town at a training seminar, while Chief Gates was attending a Brentwood fundraiser for the campaign against Proposition F, the charter amendment on police reform, all occurred on the evening the verdicts were delivered.

Although the LAPD had organizational issues and problems, and did not respond to or handle this unprecedented incident appropriately, most of the disturbance and its aftermath could have been avoided and mitigated to a large degree by an outside influence. An unexpected development and unforeseen events could have forced them to play the hand they were refusing to show.

No one knew that day that behind the scenes a mobile tactical response team—coincidentally made up of extra on-duty personnel from the nearby Lennox Sheriff's Station—stood at-the-ready. They awaited orders from their acting watch commander who earlier had initiated the formation, deployment, and game plan for this response team. The magnitude of tension building beneath the impending violence called for an immediate, decisive, and effective showing of force by law enforcement.

This response team was ready to do just that.

The sheriff's response team was poised to act on a plan with the potential not only to deflate the present escalating situation, but also to set a precedent for future events. Unfortunately, that decisive action was not taken.

As the team readied themselves, the watch commander's decision— one that might have saved lives and businesses that night—was overruled at the last second by a higher authority. That decision halted an opportunity to witness what was to be the greatest display of team work and mutual aid between law enforcement agencies ever seen in a violent and emerging civil disturbance of this magnitude.

Opportunities to engage and save face could have been seized and realized. If action had been taken, politicians, business and religious leaders, and other community figures could have launched an impetus to step in and make lasting and effective changes. This tactical response team was comprised solely of members of the Los Angeles County Sherriff's Department.

The Department could also have used a shot in the arm. As the largest Sherriff's Department and fourth largest local policing agency in the United States, the agency's image was still reeling from recent negative press and internal morale issues relating to the ARCO-NARCO incident, in which narcotics deputies and supervisors were caught stealing money and drugs from several narcotics dealers.

Never Again herein presents a true story from an angle not exploited or sensationalized by live TV. It sheds light on the primary issues contributing to the behind-the-scenes fate of the Rodney King riots response team. A jurisdictional issue and weak leadership were part of the problem, as was a decision resting on the shoulders of a sheriff's captain who lacked flexibility and was unable to see the big picture. This analysis will show how the course of history could have been changed, but for that timid decision. One person's decision had a profound effect on many.

Many of the events and experiences of the Rodney King riots on April 29, 1992, could have been prevented or at least mitigated. Events that were deadly, damaging, and disturbing, evolved into a sobering series of lessons learned not only by law enforcement, but by politicians and the communities involved. The recovery phase continues and will do so for years. It not only left its mark on law enforcement and community relations, but also on young and old members of society who felt the effects personally. The values and perceptions of those who watched the media coverage during the riots were forever changed. Race relations that many worked hard to build decades before took a step back.

Sadly, none of this had to happen....

Chapter 1
FLASH BACK

Flashback, Mid-1980s

I was a patrol training officer in West Hollywood, working the graveyard shift. At the shift briefing I was told I had an important incoming telephone call. I went over to the phone and clicked on the line on hold.

"This is Deputy Weiss." I waited for an answer, wondering who was calling and what might be so important.

It was one of my informants.

"Deputy Weiss? It's Joey."

"Hey Joey. How's it going?"

"I'm good.... Hey, ya know that guy you're looking for? The one who you got down for those robberies?" He knew I was looking for a serial street robbery suspect.

"Yeah...." My curiosity was piqued.

"Well, in 10-minutes, he'll be driving a stolen silver Dodge Charger on Kings Road." He said he could turn me on to the guy who was driving around town in a stolen silver Dodge Charger.

"Oh, yeah? How do you know?" I grabbed a pen and paper and sat forward in my chair.

He snickered. "I'll be riding with him."

"What does he look like? Can you give me his description and the car he's driving?"

Joey was an eighteen-year-old white kid from Texas, and a wannabe celebrity. He told me that he and the suspect, another young white guy, would be traveling together northbound on Kings Road from Santa Monica Boulevard to Fountain Avenue to meet with someone. My informant said he would be the front seat passenger. We quickly formulated a plan for him to bail out of the vehicle as soon as possible after I pulled the vehicle over.

My informant went serious. He was scared.

"I don't want the guy to think I snitched, Deputy. This guy will go off on me if he thinks I had anything to do with this. Everyone on the street knows how edgy he is. Nobody ever crosses him. He's like a loose cannon."

I promised the informant I would be discreet and hung up the phone. We had ten minutes to get into position. "Let's go, Larry."

I left the station with my trainee, a light-skinned African-American man who had a good heart but was failing in the patrol training program. I had recently inherited him as my partner for the next few months to give him a new start with a different training officer and to try and save his career. As we drove to the immediate area the informant said he and the suspect would be driving through, my partner and I worked out a plan to engage the suspect and stop the vehicle.

Backing the black and white radio car into an apartment complex driveway I parked to wait with the engine running. Tall palm trees and thick six-foot-high hedges gave us a vantage point in the dark, but allowed us to be hidden from passing traffic under a full moon. It was a quiet evening even with the windows down. We listened to the crickets and reviewed our game plan.

Sure enough, within minutes, the alleged stolen Dodger Charger drove directly past us through the dense residential area made up of mostly multi-story apartment complexes.

I pulled in behind the vehicle at the stop sign at Kings Road and Fountain Avenue. The driver made a left turn onto Fountain Avenue, and after checking the license plate via our radio, I initiated a traffic stop, I could see my informant sitting in the right front passenger seat. The return on the plate did indeed come back as a stolen vehicle taken in a robbery from the nearby Los Angeles Police Department Wilshire Division area.

I activated the red lights and sounded the siren. Traffic stops are dangerous. I wasn't sure what would happen next, but I was hoping we wouldn't have to initiate a chase through this residential area.

"Looks like he's pulling over," I said. "Get on the radio and give our location." My partner transmitted our location as we initiated the traffic stop.

The suspect was stopped at a red light. What would he do?

"Look, Bill! The informant is bailing from the right front passenger door. He's running toward those buildings."

I looked in the direction my partner pointed and spotted the informant. He ran into a nearby multi-level apartment complex. Surprised by his passenger's actions, the suspect-driver panicked and accelerated suddenly, driving into the opposing eastbound lanes. That was it. My partner radioed that we were in pursuit. We gave chase on westbound Fountain Avenue to southbound La Cienega Boulevard against the eastbound traffic.

We passed the famed El Palacio apartment building, screeching around the corner in pursuit of our suspect. Vehicles swerved to avoid striking the stolen vehicle as it continued southbound on La Cienega Boulevard at a high rate of speed, finally pulling out of the opposing traffic lanes. The next intersection at Holloway Drive and La Cienega Boulevard was blocked by stopped traffic. The driver had few options now.

"There he goes. Look! Over there! He's turning into the Chevron Gas Station!" shouted my partner, "Whoa! He just missed that tanker." Narrowly avoiding a tanker truck unloading his fuel order, the driver fortunately missed several pedestrians standing next to and sitting on a bench at a bus stop. They scattered to get out of the way of the speeding vehicle.

I followed him into the gas station lot. The radio car violently struck a sloped concrete bump leading from the street to the top of the sidewalk and driveway, lifting the radio car inches into the air. The trainee and I struck our heads on the radio car headliner. As it bottomed out, the radio car came down with a thunderous crash as the steel frame scraped the concrete.

The driver sped out of the gas station lot with us in pursuit. He made a sharp left turn onto Westmount Drive, a narrow and steep downhill street and lost control of the car. He crashed into a telephone pole and then slid into the rear of a large van parked and facing southbound down the hill. The telephone pole was bent at a 45-degree angle, mangled wires dangling from it. I thought he would have been severely injured in that kind of collision.

The right front passenger door opened.

"I can't believe this! He's crawling over the right front passenger seat," my partner shouted. "He's exiting on the right!"

"Let's go, Larry!" I replied. We jumped out and gave chase to the suspect who was momentarily out of our view, obstructed by the row of vehicles parked on the curb facing southbound. We chased after him by foot down the steep street. I ran down the middle of the street and my partner trainee followed on the sidewalk as we attempted to box the suspect in. Several people were walking in the path of the suspect.

"Move! Get away from him!" We yelled, motioning for them to get away from the suspect. Approaching the bottom of the street it leveled out. I had noticed at the start of the foot pursuit my partner had not put out our location on the radio, but the chase had happened so quickly it wasn't until now I could do something about it. No one knew where we were to offer back up, or even if we needed it.

My partner stumbled and fell headlong on the sidewalk right in front of me, blocking my path. Just then I spotted the suspect dart from the sidewalk and run westbound between two high rise apartment complexes.

I jumped over my partner who was down on the sidewalk and took off after the suspect.

I yelled back at him, "Larry, get back up the hill to the car radio and put out an emergency broadcast to set up a containment of the area." My goal was now to contain the suspect and stay hidden while monitoring his movements in the dark. We'd make our move to capture him when I had sufficient back up patrol units in the area. We had no idea if he was armed.

I was now separated from my partner and knew I had to play it safe. I continued chasing the suspect from a careful distance. I could hear him running in the gravel between the two buildings, but out of sight ahead of me in the darkness by about 20 to 25 yards. I jumped several fences and walls in the process of going after him.

In the stillness of the night, I heard the suspect breathing harshly. He was moving slowly behind a fenced and gated area several feet lower than the area I was in. At the same time I could feel and hear my own heart pounding like the sound of a drum. I sneaked a peek over the wall, and in the moonlight, I saw the suspect kneeling down between two bushes approximately 15-yards away and toward the back of the adjacent building. In the distance I heard the radio cars rolling from the nearby sheriff's station, sirens wailing and tires squealing.

The suspect had slowly moved to a point right below me. My adrenaline kicked into overdrive. I jumped over the wall into the adjoining complex. I corralled the suspect between the two tall apartment complexes and block walls enclosed us with a 10-foot fenced gate leading to the front street.

I screamed at the suspect. "Get on the ground! Now!" I said a lot more than that in much more colorful language.

He did just the opposite, lunging at me. We fought as the suspect attempted to pull my flashlight from my left hand. Then he grabbed for my holstered weapon. I couldn't let him take my gun. A surge of energy hit me.

"I said, get down, NOW!" I kept screaming at the suspect to comply. Expletives flew.

Tenants living in the buildings above us heard my shouts echoing through the corridor between the two apartment complexes. They called the sheriff's station. I learned later that desk personnel heard me yelling, including the expletives, at the suspect on at least one of the callers' open telephone lines and were able to pinpoint my location. Responding field units were soon on their way to assist me.

The responding radio cars were nearing. Once again he fought hard to reach my holstered weapon. A second surge of adrenaline kicked in. I knew now I was fighting for my life and I was back there alone. He was fighting to stay out of my custody and a possible prison term. The stakes were big for both of us. I struck him on the head with my flashlight. The blow made him release his grip on me and stagger on his feet. This allowed me to get him down on the ground. I handcuffed him just as the responding patrol units came to a screeching skid in the street in front of our location.

I pushed the suspect out through the wrought iron gate, hidden by a huge palm tree, into to a flurry of rotating patrol car emergency lights and shining flashlights from the other deputies creeping down the corridor between the two buildings. Looking down, I discovered my jacket and hand were covered in blood from the suspect's bleeding scalp. I had accidentally struck the fingers of my left hand with my flashlight trying to hold the suspect down with my hand. Even though my hand was throbbing intensely, I was relieved. I had survived his attack.

Just, another routine day.

Chapter 2
CALM BEFORE
THE STORM

April 29, 1992
Wednesday 6:00 AM

I awoke late, in a startled panic with a pounding headache from not enough sleep. A news talk show endlessly rehashing the Rodney King trial was blaring from my clock radio as the backup alarm clock shrieked in the background. The announcer described King's 1991 beating by the Los Angeles Police Department, blow-by-blow. He was arguing with an irate caller. I visualized the baton strikes that I and the rest of the world had seen on replay so many times.

"Those officers kicked, tasered, and mercilessly beat Mr. King. They left him with crushed—"

The radio announcer interrupted the caller. *"Come on, Ma'am, he was equally responsible for the altercation. The guy was drunk! He refused to stop when the officers tried—"*

"That is NOT the issue," the caller continued. *"Please stop interrupting me. Those cops beat him down unnecessarily! They left him with crushed bones, and shattered teeth. They kicked him so hard he had kidney damage— kidney damage! His (expletive) skull was fractured. If that man hadn't heard the sirens and captured the attack on video...."*

The argument between the radio talk show host and caller continued. I'd heard it all before many times. A few minutes passed before I realized I had set the wrong wake up time. I overslept for the first time in my career after a late and busy evening shift at the Lennox Sheriff's Station.

Other than the report of a deputy-involved traffic accident, the night unfolded as did most others. There were the usual fight calls, disturbances, arrests, and a drive-by shooting. I was the only field sergeant during the entire shift, and I also had the responsibility of supervising the patrol units for the Marina Del Rey substation area.

My total patrol coverage was approximately thirty field units, covering a diverse area of South Central Los Angeles, which included both Lennox and Marina Del Rey station areas. It was a drive of 5-10 miles to the Marina Del Rey areas from Lennox, depending upon which area the call or incident originated from. Lennox Station coverage for the field sergeant and watch commander went from Lawndale in the south, to the Athens District in the N/E, to Marina Del Rey on the N/W for supervisors.

We had to cross back and forth between LAPD, Inglewood PD, and Hawthorne PD areas to cover our areas. The 1932 and 1984 Olympic Games took place within the boundaries of South Central, near the USC campus at Exposition Park, which hosts the Los Angeles Coliseum.

Because I overslept I missed a 7 AM computer training class at the Sheriff's Academy in Whittier. It was an hour-and-a-half drive from my home in the Santa Clarita Valley and I'd never make it through traffic at that hour. It wasn't my favorite type of training anyway.

I called in to the station, just as the sun was rising, and spoke with the day shift watch commander, a long-time lieutenant who was well respected, but had some rough edges.

"Hey Lieutenant, this is Bill Weiss. I overslept and am not going to make the training class. Sorry about that. I thought I'd let you know for scheduling and training purposes."

"Hang on a minute, Bill." I was on hold for several minutes. "Okay, I penciled you in on the in-service sheet as my relief, as the PM watch commander." That would be my "reward" for missing the computer training class. They did not place just any sergeant into the watch commander's position. That at least gave me a sense of pride.

Even though I had been a sergeant in patrol for a little more than a year and a half, it was not uncommon for me to fill the watch commander spot, a position ordinarily occupied by a tenured lieutenant. The watch commander is in charge of the station on their shift and the position comes with a lot of responsibility. If problems arise and decisions need to be made, the watch commander makes the call and then reports to the captain if necessary. The command staff at the station trusted my supervisory, leadership, and tactical skills and lately I had filled that position at least once a week.

I was not unfamiliar with being given positions of responsibility. At the age of 15 I worked my first job as a restaurant busboy at a local amusement park, Six Flags Magic Mountain. The 70s were a time when what remained of a strong work ethic present in earlier generations still hung on by a thread. Magic Mountain was a fun place to work and teens were able to put a little money in their pockets during summer vacation. Older teenagers and college students often worked their first jobs there. After the summer season, they usually laid kids off for the slower winter months, but I was able to hang on as a dishwasher, mainly due to my maturity, hard work, and reliability.

In those days most people working at Magic Mountain were college students in their 20s. Over the course of a few years, I was promoted several times and eventually, at age 18, was a head supervisor. I supervised 85 people during the summers including those employed by four restaurants at the front of the amusement park.

I grasped how to run a large and full-scale operation with many responsibilities and lead people much older than myself. Because I supervised minors, I dealt with work-hour restrictions. Scheduling, time records, and employee issues all factored into my responsibilities. At the same time I juggled customer complaints, food preparation, ordering, and the handling of money. The fast pace of an amusement park and throngs of tourists added to the pressure. But I was able to handle it.

In addition to the leadership skills I learned from my work at Magic Mountain, at 16 I participated in the LEEP (Law Enforcement Explorer Program) program and graduated from the 18-week academy, which prepared me for a career in law enforcement. The experiences taught me how to focus, develop confidence, and think on my feet. It was physically and mentally demanding, especially for a 16-year-old kid.

Over the years I learned to watch people to see how they led, talked to, and dealt with others. Paying attention to the good things people did and modeling myself after them, while striving to improve, was important. I have always been a self-motivator, never wanting to disappoint others or myself, and always try to achieve and get ahead. Paying close attention to what other deputies and supervisors did, so I wouldn't make the same mistakes and could learn from a variety of people, was invaluable.

Planning ahead and doing my homework has been a hallmark throughout my life and my career. Without such planning, accomplishing goals I have set for myself would not have been possible. It seems that I have always had to work harder than most people to achieve my objectives.

As my law enforcement career progressed, I took on more responsibilities and promoted through hard work. I've made it my business to know my stuff, practice what I preached, and treat people fairly. I was pretty comfortable making decisions and taking action.

～

I got out of bed that morning and downed two Tylenol® capsules for my headache before showering. After dressing, I walked into the living room and turned on the television. All around me was the cheerful bustle of a family preparing for the day. I poured a bowl of Wheaties and sat down to watch the morning news.

There were several hours before I needed to leave for my 1:30 PM shift at work. At this point in my career, I worked a four-day work week. My schedule varied. On Sundays I worked what was called a Day-PM double shift. I started work at 5:30 AM and worked through to 1:30 PM. Then my second shift started at 1:30 PM and ended at 9:30 PM. Monday, Tuesday, Wednesday I worked from 1:30-9:30 PM. They were long days but I loved my job. I looked forward to the shorter eight- hour shift that day—or so I thought.

The same kind of discussion I heard earlier on the radio talk show was blaring from the TV as well. The controversial Rodney King case was in the process of being heard by a state court jury and a verdict was expected.

TV Newscaster:

"*The entire country awaits the verdict in the case of Rodney King, a 25-year-old unemployed construction worker with two children who was stopped by police and beaten....*

"*...the unedited, seven-minute videotape—spanning the time from King's abrupt motion to a point where he lies handcuffed, hogtied and bleeding at the side of the road....*"

"*...shows one officer swinging his nightstick at King like a baseball bat....*"

I finished my cereal and after washing my bowl, grabbed a copy of the *Los Angeles Times* sitting on the counter. The paper published updates about the twelve jurors who were still in session before rendering their verdict.

The man everyone was talking about, Rodney King, was an African-American on parole from prison on a robbery conviction. He had past convictions for assault, battery and robbery. Along with two passengers, he had been stopped in a Hyundai on March 3, 1991, on the 210 freeway in Lake View Terrace, northeast of Los Angeles.

Clocked driving up to 115 MPH while the officers were in pursuit, King was stopped for speeding, driving while intoxicated, and for failure to yield. He was also believed to be under the influence of PCP. Toxicology reports later indicated otherwise. He was however, determined to have been at 2.5 times the legal limit for alcohol at the time he was pulled over.

Two CHP officers, Timothy and Melanie Singer, a husband and wife team, were assisted by five LAPD officers: Sergeant Stacy Koon, Officers Laurence Powell, Timothy Wind, Theodore Briseno, and Rolando Solano. Theodore Briseno later testified the three other officers were out of control during this incident.

The graphic footage of the traffic stop after the high speed pursuit was being played and replayed on television. Nine minutes of film was videotaped from an apartment balcony by an amateur photographer with his clunky Sony Handycam. The video showed King resisting arrest and being beaten and tasered. King was kicked in the head and struck several times with baton strikes, all for over a minute, then tackled and struck several more times with batons after getting to his feet, and before being handcuffed by police while on the ground. This incident was the focus for media attention and a rallying point for police-abuse activists in Los Angeles and around the United States.

As a result of the beating, King suffered a fractured cheekbone, a fracture to the base of his skull, and a fractured leg. The majority of media coverage interpreted the incident as a shocking tragedy and accused the police of abusing their power.

My wife glanced at the TV screen as she came into the room. "Good morning! I'll be going to Ralph's after school today. Anything special you want?"

My mind was still on the Rodney King situation. "Nothing I can think of."

I hugged my wife and son good-bye as they were leaving to drop him off at elementary school on her way to work. Before they left, I reminded my son to behave and not to get into anything with the other kids at school. At six years old he was bigger than most kids his age and I wanted him to be responsible.

I had my own first lessons in being held accountable at an early age when I was his age. My father was also a deputy sheriff for 27 years with the LA County Sheriff's Department. He worked long hours and was mostly a patrol deputy. As I grew up he was either working, which frequently required him to be sleeping during the day after working the night shift, or going to court or some other function. I remember his absence during my childhood, something I came to understand a little better as I got older.

Although he was often working, my father was a strong influence. He taught me that discipline and hard work were important especially for school and home responsibilities. Growing up, I established the value of a strong work ethic as I usually did most of the chores, yard work, and other basic household duties. I learned to be responsible and accountable; I guess by necessity.

As my son walked to the car, I called to him. "Remember you have a soccer game on Saturday."

"I know, Dad." He waved and smiled before climbing into the back seat of my wife's car. He loved micro-soccer and I felt good that he shared some of the same interests in sports as I had when I was young.

I was involved in several youth sports as a kid. From the time I was five, my favorite sport, basketball, was a big part of my life. This early influence formed my views on teamwork and discipline. I also valued physical training as an adult. Adopting a regimen of self-care played a big part in maintaining balance between home and work.

Although my father was not able to attend most of my sports events due to work, I was glad my mother often did. Having her rooting for me from the sidelines gave me a sense of pride. Knowing she was watching made me try even harder to do my best.

I learned a lot from my coaches, which in turn inspired me to coach my son years later in many sports he was involved in. Despite having similar work hours and obligations as my father, I coached my son through 10-straight-years of youth basketball leagues from the time he was five until he was fifteen. I also assisted as a coach in soccer, baseball, and football.

I made it a point to be there for my son and to give him something I didn't always have. I was also involved in his school activities and homework. I guess things turned out okay as he graduated with a BA degree in engineering. Today, he runs his own automotive engineering company and has done so successfully for over five years.

～

The Tylenol® was finally kicking in. My headache began to subside as I took care of my daily chores. Feeling better, I decided to get in a full workout consisting of weight training and cardio vascular exercise. I put on my running shoes and finished with a three-mile jog through my neighborhood while listening to music: U2's "Mysterious Ways" and "I Still Haven't Found What I'm Looking For", Marky Marx's "Good

Vibrations," London Beat's "I've Been Thinking of You," and REM's "Losing My Religion".

I jogged through my neighborhood, appreciating the peaceful surroundings and good neighbors. They were decent, average people like most of us. Although I wasn't particularly close with all of them, there were a few I got to know pretty well. My neighbors were mostly white, but a few were people of color, including a Korean-American man across the street.

"Good Morning, John." I waved as I passed my neighbor's house. He was outside watering his lawn.

"Hi, Bill." He waved back as I passed. He was a nice man and although we didn't socialize formally, we talked now and then and greeted each other in passing.

I didn't realize it at the time, but that day would be the last time for a long time that I saw people as people, without seeing the ethnic and racial differences the next few hours and days would highlight. The divisions along lines of color and ethnicity, once fuzzy, would become clearly defined.

Panting, I finished my long run. Mentally and physically pumped up, I was ready to handle the rest of my day, or so I thought.

Chapter 3
PIVOTAL MOMENTS

After finishing my workout I showered and ate a ham sandwich for lunch before heading out to work at noon for my 1:30 PM shift. At the same time I packed my dinner in an Igloo cooler, something I usually did in those days. Our work days were unpredictable and opportunities to go out for meals were rare if I was working inside. There were no official breaks; we usually ran by the seat of our pants. I often ate my lunch or dinner while in a protected parking lot, usually in an industrial or business area, on the hood of my radio car when I was working outside in the field.

Driving to work on the never-forgiving 405 freeway I heard updated radio news reports regarding the King trial. My sixth sense told me that although no one really expected a verdict that day, something might yet be decided.

Traffic grew heavier as I passed the 101 freeway exit. I was grateful to be driving in between rush hours. Even still, the usual craziness of

LA motorists was rarely avoidable. Absent-minded drivers would cut off those directly behind them setting off a domino effect of avoidance maneuvers several cars back.

For the rest of the 90-minute drive into the station, my mind focused on the Rodney King verdict. I mentally role-played scenarios about how I would handle different situations if problems developed in the Lennox area—the South Central Los Angeles area surrounded partially by LAPD's 77th Division—and the Inglewood Police Department.

During my years at Lennox Station I was no stranger to violence. I was transferred there in 1990 after being promoted to sergeant and stayed through 1994. It was a busy station in an area with a high crime rate. Robberies, assaults, and deadly shootings were daily events. Gunfire was commonplace. Lennox Station averaged more than one murder a week in 1992.

Prior to my years at the Lennox Station many experiences shaped my career as a deputy sheriff. The fact that I was involved in a variety of incidents, including a lot of foot pursuits, vehicle pursuits, and containments strengthened my confidence in my ability to handle stressful and chaotic incidents and situations.

As a deputy, working patrol in West Hollywood between 1983 and 1987, I dealt with a variety of crimes and situations, including a number of street robberies, assaults, and shootings. The gangs would come up La Cienega and La Brea and commit two or three robberies over a period of a couple of hours. We would hear over the radio they were in one area and then a few minutes later, had stolen a car or committed a robbery in another.

I had been in West Hollywood for four years by 1987. I remember one particular incident occurred when there were 45-minutes left of my last shift before transferring to the Pre-Employment, Backgrounds Investigation unit. Prior to this incident, there were 21 street robberies committed over a period of two-months, a few in our area, but mostly in LAPD's areas. Law enforcement officers were out chasing the suspects, but no one could find them. A few weeks prior, an off-duty custody deputy from the jail was the victim of an attempted robbery and was involved in a shooting with the suspects. So it was a time of pretty unusual intensity among the LAPD and LASD. We wanted these guys caught.

I had been focusing constantly on these incidents and had occasional contact with LAPD officers to keep abreast of their latest information. I had my eye out for the suspects and had been looking hard.

This particular evening, I was driving down Melrose Ave, out of our area by a couple blocks. I happened to look down a side street in a residential area—actually an alley behind a restaurant—and I saw tail lights of a car double-parked in the street. As would often happen during my career, a sixth sense that comes with experience hit me and I thought, these are the guys – there's something up. I knew it.

I hurriedly looped around another street and went back down an alley behind the restaurant. As I reached the street my partner and I could see the car in question taking off in the distance. Several people were yelling, "They just robbed us! There's four of them. They went down that way!"

I hit the gas hard and drove down the street in the direction pointed out by the victims. When the suspects saw us coming they sped down the street two blocks, turning a corner. We were right behind them, tires screaming. We rounded the corner and saw all four doors were open as the car was parked in the middle of the street with the engine running. The suspects had abandoned the car and ran in different directions to hide in the residential neighborhood.

An LAPD unit heard my broadcast and responded. They hooked up one of the suspects as he ran across the street in front of their radio car. A few minutes later, an LAPD helicopter hovered overhead and spotted one of the suspects in a backyard inside the containment area. Later during a grid search a K-9 dog located the other two suspects, also inside our containment. Bad guys really don't like those dogs. We were able to get all four suspects.

On my final night as a patrol deputy in 1987, it felt good nailing the suspects that were now responsible for 22 street robberies. The next few years would provide their own brand of drama, culminating in the biggest challenge of my career—the LA riots.

Daily work life didn't change much after I got to Lennox Station in 1990, except maybe for the worse. The gangs didn't have to travel far to get to our jurisdiction area. Many were already there.

I was a patrol sergeant at the time of and before the riots. During one shift I remember, at 1:30 PM a multijurisdictional task force was working a surveillance operation for an assault with a deadly weapon suspect.

The task force members were all from different agencies. One or two were LASD personnel. They were sitting in cars in surveillance mode in our area when a gang drive-by-shooting went down right in front of them.

We were in the middle of a shift change and I was just coming on duty. Immediately after the shooting, the officers and deputies were involved in a foot pursuit. They gave out two different locations spread out by a block or two, where the shootings occurred during the foot pursuit. A suspect was shot and down on the sidewalk at one location when residents in the mostly black apartment complex were hanging out of their apartment windows yelling profanities at us. It was a wild scene. Someone even tried to take the suspect's gun, which was lying on the ground next to him, inside the crime scene on the sidewalk.

This happened right before the riots. Citizen against cop no matter what—that was the overall mindset. People would try to take evidence from a crime scene or intercede into the problem so we had to be on top of it.

In this incident we had undercover officers from different law enforcement agencies involved in two different shootings at two different locations—in both cases, unrelated to what they were there for. Trying to contain these two different crime scenes where officers were involved in separate shootings was bad enough, but one became a homicide scene, requiring a tighter control of the scene for responding homicide and coroner investigators.

Lennox Station also covered the more affluent Marina Del Rey area, so as a field sergeant, the coverage area was large. If something went down there—a shooting, a crash, a use-of-force, or a citizen's complaint, we had to drive over there and handle it. Then if something happened closer to the station, we'd have to turn around and get back there to handle that incident. Every night was different and we never knew what was going to happen. There was a lot of bouncing around. We boomeranged from crisis to crisis. In fact, crises were routine.

The thought of civil unrest was on my mind during my drive to work on April 29th. I thought back to my patrol training days when we formed skirmish lines for protests at the Federal Building in Westwood. Halloween during the West Hollywood Halloween Carnival was another big one. It's the largest Halloween street party in the world, and it happens in West Hollywood every year on October 31st. Half a million people take to the streets of Santa Monica Boulevard to enjoy the wild costumes, and be a part of uninhibited and often rowdy crowds.

Even when people gathered for fun, things could get out of hand. The mostly gay Halloween celebrants would close Santa Monica Boulevard attempting to rock and tip over one or two Rapid Transit District buses for thrills. As I continued driving to work, I replayed the desktop training scenarios in the incident command classes I had attended at the Emergency Operations Bureau under the nationally known expert, Lieutenant Sidney Bowers. These tabletop role-playing exercises were usually no-win situations. We were faced with one hypothetical disaster or incident after another to challenge us to react, plan ahead, and think on our feet, along with using sound tactical knowledge and procedures. We were well trained to handle any eventuality.

Wednesday, 1:30 PM

Upon arriving at work and changing into my uniform, I relieved the day shift watch commander. About twenty minutes into my shift, I started to hear word through the media and executive staff members, including phone calls from different Court Services personnel, that the King jurors might reach a decision later in the afternoon. This was only the seventh day of deliberations. Lennox station was just a short distance from the Los Angeles International Airport and when a plane flew overhead, they occasionally flew in so close above us the station shook and more often than not, we could hardly hear each other speak. Not today. Everybody had an opinion and was determined to be heard. I was not the only one who felt a menacing sense of dread. Police action seemed inevitable.

A low-level hysteria rose throughout the station as the afternoon wore on. I studied my in-service sheet and my available on-duty personnel and was surprised to find extra personnel assigned to the PM shift. This was due to the fact that many people had not been assigned to attend any training classes. Wednesdays were our typical training day and extra personnel were built into the monthly schedule to accommodate absences as we met our constant training requirements.

"Hey Sergeant," one of the desk officers called out to me as I passed.

"Hello, Tom."

"So what do you think of this Rodney King trial? Do you think they're going to reach a verdict today?"

"I don't know. It's possible," I said, even though with every passing minute I was surer   they would.

"How do you think it will go?"

"I guess it could go either way, based on the evidence." I was hoping for justice to be done.

No one was sure what the verdicts might be, although we all speculated. I saw a lot of troubled faces, recognizing the strange sense of foreboding I felt among all of us. I knew it would be better to be organized than to be caught off guard. As watch commander it was my responsibility to take whatever action would be needed. Crowd control situations were complex and dangerous. I set about preparing to respond to any emergency.

Wednesday, 1:50 PM

I formulated a plan to deal with any hostile reaction the verdicts might create within the community and in the media. I arranged for Watch Sergeant, Jay McKenzie—a well-built hard worker with a razor-sharp crew cut—to gather our riot-response gear, just in case. I respected and trusted him highly, as he had prior SWAT (Special Weapons and Tactical Team) experience when he was assigned to the Special Enforcement Bureau. He also had the station collateral duty of making sure the station armory was always ready.

Wednesday, 2:00 PM

After finalizing my plan we discussed several possible issues and personnel matters that might arise if we responded to any disturbances or violent situations. As I discussed my plan with Jay, I felt some anxiety and tension. We both knew the likelihood was high that we would be involved in something dangerous in our area during the course of the evening, and the best way to handle anything that would boil up was to be prepared.

"My plan will allow us to continue patrolling and covering our station area with our normal patrol deployment and resources," I explained. "At the same time, we can use the extra personnel not assigned to attend training today as our mobile tactical response team."

"I agree, Bill. We'll send them wherever we need them."

I nodded and continued, "Let's plan to use the entire station mobile response team available—Field Sergeants Randy Webb and George Anton. Randy is a seasoned veteran."

Anton was only in his third day in patrol as a sergeant and assigned to ride with Webb in the same supervisory car-30S.

"I'm thinking we should go with three more two-man training cars, and one two-man experienced car assigned to the Vermont/Athens District."

Jay leaned in and listened closely as I pointed to locations on the map in front of us. We both knew that every step in the sequence of our response had to be precise if this plan was going to work. "In the Central District, the area immediately around the station, we'll use five single-man radio cars. They can be available for a separate mobile response deployment if needed."

In all, I reserved a total of ten radio cars and fifteen total personnel for any mobile tactical emergency response. I decided not to double-up personnel in some single-man cars. I wanted to make our deployment numbers appear greater than they actually were out in the field, and to allow us to be more mobile and flexible.

"Since they're without an immediate field supervisor, we'll leave seasoned deputies in the smaller Central District squad."

Jay paused and after a deep breath, he nodded confidently. "I think this is a solid strategy. I agree with your reasoning, Bill."

The actual station facility was also staffed with two extra jailers, armed and stationed separately in the front and rear of the building to provide extra security. Our typical deployment of field personnel included seven two-man, five single-person patrol units and the inside station, desk, jailer, and administrative personnel, who were all positioned and deployed as usual. The station was designated as the staging area for the second and smaller response team in the Central District area. I felt confident that we would be covered.

TV news continued to broadcast alarm in the background.

Wednesday, 2:45 PM

The station desk Watch Deputy, Tony Everett, was a trusted and experienced training officer. I briefed Everett and the other inside personnel on what my plans would be regarding the staging and deploying of the main mobile field response team at Los Angeles County Fire Station No. 14, which was across the street from Washington High School at the corner of Normandie Avenue and 108th Street.

Built in 1949, Fire Station No. 14 was listed on the National Register of Historic Places in 2009. The three-story building was the second of two all-black segregated fire stations in Los Angeles and a source of community pride.

I also briefed personnel about the second and smaller response team located closer to the station. I picked the Vermont/Athens District location to centralize a larger response to potential problem areas I guessed might arise mostly due to demographics and past history. My watch sergeant and watch deputy were in agreement with my plan. It gave me a vote of confidence and made me feel even more certain about my proposed deployment strategy.

I then briefed the two field sergeants by telephone, who then updated the field deputies about the general pre-staging idea and mobile tactical response plan. We would be ready if anything developed after the LAPD verdicts were announced. Response gear, which included AR-15 assault rifles and tear gas were gathered along with camcorders, extra ammunition, shields, and helmets. They were ready to be picked up and to be delivered later to the response teams if needed.

I hoped we'd never need to spring into action.

Wednesday 3:00 PM

The afternoon wore on with breathless media reports churning what little information was available about the verdicts. Calls from concerned citizens and others added to tension and anxiety throughout the station, among both the sworn and civilian staff. We were being warned. A troubling dynamic began to present itself as several of the African-American female secretarial staff members at the station began making sarcastic and snide remarks to the white deputies going about their business inside the station. These surprising comments were coming from the same civilian staff members with whom we worked side-by-side for years. Never before had they challenged or questioned the ethics, honesty, or intent of the sworn staff members. Everybody was on edge and it showed.

What would happen next? The impending decision of 12 people held the answers. We had a short time to prepare and at the same time, several minutes ticked by. People had an eye on the television and an ear to the radios that played in every office.

Chapter 4

SHADOW WARRIORS

Wednesday 3:15 PM

The verdicts were in. We braced ourselves.

Over live television on that warm Wednesday afternoon, on the seventh day of jury deliberations, the jury, consisting of ten whites, one Hispanic, and one Asian, from the Simi Valley courthouse in Ventura County, delivered not-guilty verdicts. On one officer the jury failed to reach a verdict on the use of excessive force. The officers were acquitted of all assault charges.

A grim hush, especially among the civilian professional staff, including several of the African-American secretaries, took hold of the station. The breaking television news alerts ripped through the silence as some of the civilian staff muttered harsh words. Within the hour, an angry crowd outside the courthouse soon swelled to more than 300—most of them protesting what they saw as unjust verdicts.

Wednesday, 4:00 PM

During the next two hours, community activists and leaders urged calm, even as rage and resentment built. A strong cloud of animosity rested heavily, like a foggy beach day, over the station. The white sworn personnel and black civilian personnel were pitted against each other. The same people we worked with shoulder-to-shoulder for years, distanced themselves from us, the white sworn staff. A terrible feeling soured my gut, telling me this was going to be a long night in many ways, and not just inside the station.

~

Later in the afternoon, Hyungwon Kang, a Korean-American photo-journalist for the Los Angeles Times was on his way home from the office when the LAPD scanner in his company vehicle caught his attention. A few minutes later, he heard one of his fellow photographers was stranded near the intersection of Florence and Normandie, and Kang went to his rescue. As he drove into the battle zone, his car was pelted with bricks and bottles. Kang covered the riots for three days and nights, taking powerful pictures that documented what was going on in that part of the city. He also had insight into what was going on with LAPD and why it would later be reported they were nowhere to be found. He described what he saw when interviewed at a later date.

"In the late afternoon, I heard on the LAPD scanner for all units to evacuate the Florence and Normandie area. People had already broken into some stores and they were pulling stuff out of there. And as soon as I approached with my camera and started taking pictures, some people were coming out of nowhere with baseball bats and started chasing me. So I had no choice but to run back to the car and we had to evacuate from those situations.

On the second day, there was just ongoing smoke and fire coming out of Koreatown especially, so I started focusing on the Koreatown area especially. I came upon one supermarket on Western and 5th that was still intact and there were armed volunteers who came to save the shop from looters." His final statement has sadly proven to be true in similar events throughout history.

"Well, twenty-years after the riots," laments Kang, *"the suffering still goes on."*

Wednesday, 5:00 PM

More than two dozen LAPD police officers commanded by Lieutenant David Forest of the 77th Street Division, were confronted by growing throngs of protesters near Florence and Normandie Avenues in South Central Los Angeles. These officers had responded to a radio call of fellow officers involved in a foot pursuit nearby. After the suspect was captured, officers were met by a hostile crowd that pelted them with bricks, bottles, and other debris. LAPD, outnumbered, retreated and left the area. Lieutenant Forest briefly returned a second time on orders from the Captain of 77th Street Division, Pat Malone. Lieutenant Forest ordered his patrol units back to their command post, later discovered to be at 54th Street at Van Ness Avenue and at Arlington Avenue. Lieutenant Forest assessed it was unsafe to send officers in. He ordered them not to respond to any emergency calls. They did not return to the scene of violence and chaos. At the same time, 911 emergency operators continued to broadcast emergency calls to 77th Street Division patrol cars, but received no acknowledgements or responses.

The Breaking News Reports continued. A male reporter, Robert, recounted a terrifying experience to a female newscaster. He was highly emotional:

"This car pulled up and started screaming at us and throwing full bottles of beer at our truck. Needless to say we turned the corner and got out of there quickly."

The female newscaster asked:

"Robert, what were they screaming?"

He replied, *"Long live Rodney King ... justice for Rodney King ... and other things we probably can't say. Obviously, the anger, the hostility, the bitterness ... those feelings are there and it seems that the anger is building."*

Female Newscaster:

"Could you tell if they were reacting to you as a member of the news media or if they were reacting to you as a white man?"

Robert:

"It's hard to tell. Maybe we look like police officers in the truck, I don't know. I tried to smile and wave ... and I saw the anger and the fury in their faces."

∾

LAPD Captain Malone pulled back from the flash point intersection when he determined there were too many protesters and it would be too dangerous and tactically unsound to engage. The crowd was venting its anger on passing motorists. LAPD officers at the command post stood angry and frustrated, waiting for orders as the initial stages of the riot began to rage out of control. Orders were given then cancelled and officers were told to stand by for another plan.

All of these incidents were unbeknownst to me as the watch commander at Lennox Station. I observed the television news reports on every available channel with a sinking sense of dread. ABC, Channel 7 showed a video shot from a helicopter directly above the Florence and Normandie intersection. Seeing a police car the reporter described the situation below.

"I'm going to lose him; I'm going right over him now, but honestly this is the first law enforcement activity I've seen out here."

In the TV Studio a male newscaster replied, *"They obviously have thought about this. They anticipated this—they meaning the LAPD. They obviously have plans to deal with it. And as we said before they've allocated a million dollars to overtime in case things like this happen ... so they are obviously carrying out a pre-thought-out plan."*

Were they? Really? It didn't appear that way. I was dumbfounded watching the situation spin out of control.

The helicopter camera panned the streets, showing the protesters who appeared to own the turbulent intersection.

Then a female newscaster said, *"In the meantime, don't go near this area—South Central Los Angeles at Florence and Normandie, because there is still no police presence there and a lot of people trying to get through that intersection have been assaulted with rocks and bottles and sticks. So, as long as it's an on-going situation, you are best-advised to stay clear."*

Coming from a helicopter, the video footage was a little shaky, but there was no mistaking the escalation of violence with every passing minute. Anger seemed to fuel more of the same and spin into violence and chaos. I started thinking the breaking news reports were doing more harm than good. It was almost a commercial for pinpointing the location to come to for people who were at home and wanted to do something, and be a part of the exciting action.

The male newscaster commented:

"Help me Ann, let's recap what we've seen. We've seen a liquor store and a gas station continue to be looted ... rocks and various things thrown at school busses ... RTD busses...."

The female newscaster, whose name I presume was Ann, piped in. *"We've seen two people dragged from cars in this intersection—one woman pulled from her car and into the street."*

She continued, *"Somebody just threw a bottle rocket!"*

"The people who are being allowed to drive through this intersection are really in grave danger and I'll say it again, I wonder why these streets have not been blocked off as of yet. You would think they would not expose seemingly innocent people to this kind of violence."

They, I thought. *I know who they're talking about—The LAPD.*

What was LAPD doing, allowing this to billow up into complete pandemonium? What were they thinking? Where were they?

Female newscaster:

"Hopefully the word is getting out on all of the radio stations in town too." And then speaking to the public who might be watching TV she said, "If you drive around and listen to your car radio you'll get the word to stay away from this area."

Was she kidding? That was part of the problem. Unless people were watching TV or listening to their car radios, most of the city was unaware of what was going on, and those driving close to Florence and Normandie had no idea of the war zone they were about to enter or they surely would not have done so.

I thought of parents picking their kids up from afterschool programs in the area. Some were just blocks away and most were probably oblivious to the danger they might be driving into. The safety of my own wife and son many miles away came to mind and strengthened my resolve to do what was necessary for the safety of innocent bystanders.

Phone calls continued to flood the station desk indicating an escalation in activity and minor disturbances in the nearby areas of LAPD. I decided it was time to up the ante and prepare for a possible tactical engagement.

This chaos was going to go one of two ways at this point. The unrest would either dissipate after a few hours of people letting off steam, or we would have a full blown city-wide riot on our hands. I was hoping for the former, but everything pointed toward the latter—large scale, at that.

I prepared myself to deal with whatever was coming. The heat under my collar was intensifying, and tension in the station was crackling. I reassured myself. I knew I had a solid plan in place and I trusted my skills and experience to implement it. Hopefully my plan would avert the need for riot control measures and we would be able to minimize the number of serious incidents or injuries.

I ordered the response gear assembled at the station to be delivered to the planned staging area in the Athens/Vermont District. I also ordered the Athens/Vermont District response team to meet there immediately. Then I changed course and ordered the second and smaller response team, which was assembled closer to the station, to respond to the Fire Station No. 14 command post on Normandie Avenue and join Sergeant Webb's response team. I telephoned Sergeant Webb to let him know that I was increasing his manpower with the same game plan in mind. He received the news calmly but I had a good sense he was feeling the same anxiety and dread that I was.

If necessary, I was preparing to make the bold call to engage out of our area. Jurisdiction is closely guarded in law enforcement. Decision-making in the face of the unknown and unexpected is stressful, but I trusted my ability to navigate the escalating situation. Deciding to gamble, I put my response teams together to make the most immediate and lasting impact, and to assure the best chance of success in quelling any disturbance.

I knew I would probably have only one shot at a successful engagement with the resources on hand. The mobile response team still did not include the normal patrol deployment of personnel in our own patrol areas. As I gave the above orders, the eyes and faces of the inside station staff shone with a grim seriousness and pride. They knew what was at stake.

～

Far north of Lennox Station, civilian Lee Exton was working in Sherman Oaks and on his way to his company's softball game when he heard about the building riot activity.

"We played in North Hollywood. I had the news on ... and I knew they were having problems down in South Central. I didn't realize that the rioting and violence was going to get more widespread.

I parked my car by the field. Two black ladies saw me and just started yelling at me ... yelled all kinds of names at me as if this was all my fault ... how the white man was the cause of all their problems, like I had been the one who had done everything wrong. It just got really out of hand.

About the second inning of the game the park officials came out and told us we needed to go home because the condition had gotten a lot worse and the riots had gotten closer and they were fearing for our safety. On the way home I could see fires burning on either side of the freeway; smoke blowing across the freeway ... plumes of smoke as far as you could see in either direction.

The next morning I had to go back into work, checked the news and there were still fires burning. For that whole week we were let out of work early, before dark, and asked to get home and be with our families."

Exton was among many who found themselves caught up in the fallout of verdicts that were unacceptable by a community that felt oppressed for decades. As it turned out, he and his co-workers would be among the lucky ones. The confrontation he experienced at the park was mild in comparison to what hundreds of other innocent people were experiencing in South Central.

Wednesday 6:30 PM

Several hundred angry demonstrators had gathered outside LAPD's headquarters at Parker Center in downtown Los Angeles. Police Chief Daryl Gates greeted them with an announcement.

"My officers are dealing with the situation calmly, maturely, and professionally."

He then drove to a Brentwood reception and fundraiser for the campaign against Charter Amendment F, a police reform ballot measure dealing with term limits. He finally returned to the Emergency Response Center at about 8:30 PM, long after the riots had raced across the city.

From the watch commander's office I monitored television news reports of growing and unruly crowds at LAPD headquarters at Parker Center and at the intersection of Florence and Normandie Avenues. The TV news media was, of course there to cover it—and sensationalize it.

Male Newscaster: *"We're told something else major is developing now. Back to Parker Center—Jody Baskerville? Is everything still peaceful there? Jody can you hear me? We're told something is developing there."*

There was no answer from the reporter at Parker Center so the newscaster recapped what had gone on that afternoon, *"Earlier today there were several hundred demonstrators ... pelting riot police with rocks and bottles ... we're told by our producer, something is happening there, we're not sure what."*

I had my desk personnel alert the field units on the recent swell of activity. Live TV was both beneficial and detrimental. On one hand, the live video showed what was happening, which was a good thing for those who needed a bird's eye view of the situation as the riots unfolded. On the other hand, the drama created by the news media in their quest to tell an exciting story and provide good visuals for their viewers probably added to the emotional upheaval perpetuating the violence. I often wonder how much the media contributed to the mass hysteria and how things would have gone were there not panicky play-by-play coverage.

Inside the station we felt powerless watching the events escalate into rioting bedlam. Neither law enforcement nor public officials had any idea of the madness that was about to grip South Central Los Angeles as night began to fall.

Wednesday, 6:45 PM

When there were no new incidents to film and report, TV reporters churned scenes that had occurred earlier in the day, looping them over and over to keep the excitement building. By this time, residents of Los Angeles were no longer the sole observers. The entire world was focused on South Central and the buildup of activity at the intersection of Florence and Normandie.

Unaware of the situation that awaited him, Larry Tarvin, a 52-year-old white truck driver, entered the intersection of Florence and Normandie. By the time he saw the rioters, it was too late. He was viciously dragged from his truck and beaten—a horrifying vision for those watching in real time. On a videotape of the incident an onlooker can be heard yelling. "Now you know what Rodney King felt like, white boy. ... No f***ing pity for the white man."

Fortunately, Tarvin survived. The day after he was mercilessly beaten he was interviewed in his home by the media. His body looked as though it had been dragged through a bed of broken glass and sharp-edged rocks. He had hundreds of cuts and bruises from head to toe. Tarvin's arms were crossed over several painful cracked ribs. There were seven stitches above his right eye and a bashed-in nose. I'm sure most ordinary people watching from home had never seen the physical ramifications of this kind of abuse.

"People started throwing bottles at my windows," a soft-spoken Tarvin said. "The next thing I knew they pulled me out of the truck, threw me on the ground and started kicking me."

Interviewer: "Was there any chance to escape?"

"No, none whatsoever."

Interviewer: "Did you ever fight back?"

Larry: "No. They were bigger than I am."

Interviewer: "Any idea how long this beating lasted?"

"No. I lost all track of time."

The reporter asked Tarvin why he didn't know what was going on—wasn't he listening to his radio?

"I didn't know what was going on." He had no radio in the truck.

Like so many others, Tarvin was just a guy who found himself in the wrong place at the wrong time.

While I was watching the Channel 13 KCOP helicopter broadcast continuous footage, one of the most startling images of the riots evolved. As if it weren't disturbing enough to watch rioters rise up against innocent merchants breaking windows and destroying property, something more gruesome and frightening was about to shock the toughest of live television viewers. Even at the time of this writing, anyone who was watching television that day likely still recognizes the scene the world watched unfold in living color.

Behind Larry Tarvin's white box truck in the intersection was the next victim. Like Tarvin, he had no idea what he was driving into. An act of kindness had put him in harm's way.

Video cameras honed in on a truck driver, later identified as 36-year-old Reginald O. Denny, as he was pulled from his sand-and-gravel semi-truck cab by a frenzied mob near Tarvin's truck. He had stopped his truck to avoid running over someone and the rioters were instantly on him.

Helicopters hovered over the intersection of Florence and Normandie. Looters and those setting fires and destroying property were caught in the act on film, yet still LAPD was nowhere to be found. The mob was in control. There was no police presence making any attempt to curtail the violence.

On camera the truck driver was repeatedly beaten by four male African-American suspects: Henry Watson, Antoine Walker-Miller, Gary Williams, and Damian Williams who were all 8-Trey Gangster Crips.

They smashed his skull in with a brick, tire iron, and fire extinguisher as news helicopters hovered above, recording every blow. Apparently proud of their actions, the assailants paraded around in the street and at least one raised his hand triumphantly as if they were victorious in a prize fight. As Denny was left moaning in pain on the ground, one of the assailants walked up and rifled through the unconscious man's pockets, then sprinted away with his wallet.

At the same time, a nearby liquor store, Tom's Liquor, was being looted and other white passersby fled a barrage of rocks and bottles. Most of the attacks were on Korean-American-owned businesses. Tom's Liquor Store, was one of a couple hundred liquor stores looted, burned or vandalized during the riots. Lawyer Stephen Jones, who represented many Korean-American store owners, said there was just "one black owner who had been burned out as compared to the couple of hundred Korean owners."

Jones also said some stores were saved by people putting up signs in the window reading *Black Owned*. The rioters would pass them by. Of the more than 200 liquor stores destroyed in the riots, only a few dozen were rebuilt. One of them is still open at the time of this writing: Tom's Liquor, at the corner of Florence and Normandie. Other merchants, financially devastated, never reopened.

Even with all this going on, no LAPD officers were in sight and none were seen responding as the Channel 13 News helicopter panned out into the surrounding area and then back into the intersection. In the station my fellow officers and I looked at each other, aghast. Viewers at home and around the nation were asking—as were the media—where is the LAPD?

My telephone was ringing off the hook in the watch commander's office. One call in particular moved me deeply. A woman, crying and hysterical, pleaded for me to send deputies into the area of Florence and Normandie Avenues since the LAPD was not responding. Just as previous callers had done, she praised the Sheriff's Department and said even though it was not our area, the residents wanted our help. The woman told me again and again that the community respected us and needed us. Especially, since we were located so close to the

Florence and Normandie intersection. She begged me to do something about Denny.

Moments earlier I had already entertained the risky possibility of sending in my response team to rescue Denny from the intersection. My plan was to deploy the team Code 3 with red lights and sirens and to encircle the scene where Denny was lying. Ten radio cars would surround the scene where Denny was lying in the configuration of a semi-circle. An arrest and rescue team of three deputies and two sergeants would then rescue him. This left ten deputies back at the radio cars armed with shotguns and AR-15's, protecting the entire rescue team. The flashpoint at Florence and Normandie Avenues was only one mile and thirteen city blocks away from our jurisdictional boundary. I had complete faith in the team's ability to safely and quickly rescue Denny and get out.

This phone call from the woman pleading with me to do something was all I needed to make an extraordinarily political and daring decision. I thanked the woman for her call and before I hung up, I told her I couldn't guarantee anything but would see what I could do to help. Her words rang in my ears.

It's an honor and also a great feeling to be reminded that the people you are protecting trust you and the way you do things. Law enforcement is demanding work. One of the most difficult parts of the job is dealing with internal politics and personnel issues. A variety of people in different positions need to come together as part of a team. People are at different skill levels and they have different temperaments. A leadership position requires patience and the ability to organize team members to get the job done. I didn't minimize the difficulty of implementing my plan.

It can be very challenging working with minimally competent people. You have to work with what you have and that can be difficult, especially in emergent and life and death situations. You have to be on top of things when working with people who are not performing up to par.

Dealing with internal politics and corruption, I found later in my career, to be more troubling and daunting than dealing with the public or criminals. Interfacing with politicians and citizens-on-a-mission could be frustrating. Sometimes people wanted us to do things that were just not feasible. It could be challenging to diplomatically explain the way things work to people who watch TV programs where things get solved in an hour. Those things just don't happen in real life.

I had already decided to act on my plan before I concluded my conversation with the panicking caller. Watching Denny still being pummeled toughened my resolve. I walked toward the dispatch center, determined to activate the response team. Through the large one-way glass window overlooking the front counter and lobby of the station, I saw my station commander heading toward my office.

Captain Chet Monroe, an African-American man of a medium build and short graying hair, had been the unit commander of Lennox Station for several years and was nearing retirement. He was a fairly quiet presence, rarely visible around the station. I quickly briefed him on the media reports, news helicopter footage, and other intelligence I had received, including the Denny beating that was unfolding on television. I explained how I formed a response team to deploy from our extra regular patrol personnel. He was aware of the lack of any kind of response by LAPD—anywhere in the riot-torn areas. I talked fast explaining the personnel I had put into place, using both the Athens/Vermont and Central area response teams, emphasizing that our regular station area field deployment coverage would still be intact—including inside and extra station security.

He was silent, listening to the TV, while my heart pounded. I went on to tell Captain Monroe about my plan and my confidence that it would be successful with minimal risk to our personnel. I emphasized, due to my training and experience, we needed to contain this situation immediately before it worsened. I stopped before I started repeating myself.

I then asked him to give the order to deploy the mobile response team.

I waited for his response. And I waited.

He stared in a daze at the television inside my office watching the mob surge back and forth, Denny on the ground. Swallowing hard, Captain Monroe paused and quietly said that we would not be going outside of our area and sending deputies into LAPD's area. He said, "We are standing down."

The next few moments felt like an eternity. I could feel the blood in my face heat up and I began to sweat. I felt as though I had been stabbed in the chest. Standing down? No. No. Couldn't he see what was happening? We could do something about this. It was the right and humane thing to do.

It would have taken me thirty-seconds to walk over to the desk and order the emergency response team to deploy. I was that close to countermanding his order before he walked in. It took effort to stop myself doing just that. But I was a police officer veteran and obeying orders was engrained in me.

I wanted to argue. I wanted to remind him how the Sheriff's Department had just gone through turmoil and embarrassment with the Arco-Narco scandal in which several members of the elite Narcotics Division had been caught extorting and skimming money and stealing narcotics from suspects during big drug busts. This would be a shot in the arm and morale-booster for the entire department. Deputies' photographs would headline the front page of the *Los Angeles Times* showing LASD saving a bloody Reginald Denny in the middle of LAPD's jurisdiction. I imagined the news reports headlines after we rescued Denny, assisted the other assault victims, and took control of the intersection.

Implementing the strategy I had devised, might possibly have changed the course of history from what was about to emerge over the course of the next several days. Instead, business owners who had invested their lives in building their businesses were on the brink of loss while innocent people were living their final hours.

Chapter 5
DREAMING

My mind soared away from the captain and the television. Tuning him out, I floated away into my own world. I had stepped out of myself, for what I realized later, was only seconds; however, it gave me a momentary halt to avoid throwing away my career in a furious argument with the captain—that I would lose.

I visualized myself walking over to the desk personnel, as if the Captain had never arrived, calling the field sergeant and giving orders to deploy the emergency response team. I saw myself tell Sergeant Webb, at the fire station staging area, the specifics of my plan to rescue Denny and to take the intersection back from the mob.

I advised Sergeant Webb this was a one shot deal and told him to be decisive and aggressive. If the rioters allowed us to control the intersection, we should hold it. If we couldn't hold it, we should get in and out quickly, grab the truck driver and get any other victims out of there, and retreat along with the response team. I told him this could be a do-or-die action and that I had faith in him. Signing off, I wished him good luck.

I envisioned Sergeant Webb quickly bringing the deputies and Sergeant Anton together into a huddle in the driveway of the fire station. They would know and feel the significance of embarking on this extraordinary rescue mission.

Sergeant Webb knew they would be on camera at every moment. This is how it would go down. They would roll Code 3, with red lights and sirens, in a tight radio car single file formation and form a containment circle in the intersection with their radio cars. Each bookman would stay with the vehicle, taking cover with their shotguns and AR-15 assault rifles.

Webb fully informed his team this operation would include all ten radio cars, with ten personnel used for cover behind each radio car, and five who would efficiently and quickly execute the rescue. If other law enforcement assistance arrived—or if Sergeant Webb felt it safe to stay gauged by the crowd's behavior and actions—he would take control of the intersection by expanding their radio car containment circle and pushing the crowd out to the edges of the intersection.

One radio car and two deputies would leave immediately with any rescued person. If the intersection could not be taken back, then the entire response team would leave as they arrived. As the quick briefing and huddle dispersed, I imagined the looks in the deputies' eyes. They would feel empowered and energized, honored to be part of a daring rescue mission.

I pictured them quickly preparing their weapons and response gear and forming their radio cars into a single file line. Sergeant Webb then radioed the Sheriff's Communications Center and indicated that Lennox Station was rolling ten patrol units Code 3 to the flash point of Florence and Normandie to assist LAPD. The response from the radio room was awe-inspiring. Cheers rose up in the background from everyone present in the radio room. The news would spread like wildfire. Finally, someone, somewhere in law enforcement was taking aggressive police action. This moment was the opportunity to use my authority and command to do something positive and extraordinary.

From the fire station, a procession of ten radio cars raced northbound on Normandie Avenue; 34 short city blocks and 2½ miles in a straight line to the flash point. With precise timing and speed each intersection was quickly cleared by the lead car. Pedestrians and citizens stood back as LASD cars rolled by in a show of force.

I listened intently to the radio car traffic, monitoring the tactical response and rescue operation. Controlling this one intersection could change the momentum of the civil disturbance. The same strategy used in some past military battles where the control of one town, one hilltop, one beach, or one bridge had changed the course of a battle.

I began humming and whispering the lyrics to Phil Collins song, "In the Air Tonight," to calm myself and help me focus. I heard Sergeant Webb advise the Sheriff's Communication Center (SCC) over the radio that they were rolling into LAPD's area, per the Lennox Watch Commander. Other sheriff's stations listened to the radio with mounting tension cheering us on.

My vision continued, seeing media helicopters picking up the procession of radio cars. They reported the way the lead unit, after clearing the large major intersections, tailed off and joined the back of the line.

Hearing the radio traffic from the nearby Firestone Station, a Special Enforcement Bureau (SEB) team of three SWAT deputies took off in a helicopter. Firestone Station was roughly the same distance and due east from the flash point. They radioed they would be providing air support and had an estimated time of arrival of three to four minutes to the flash point. Hearing that the LASD Air unit with SEB personnel on board was also engaging reassured me—and also the responding field units and the entire Lennox patrol station—that we could pull off the strategy we were putting into play.

As the response team entered LAPD's area at Manchester Boulevard they knew they would be engaging quickly. Just south of Manchester Blvd at 87th Street was the dividing line between LAPD and LASD jurisdictional areas. The flash point was now only one mile—thirteen city blocks—away at that point. Sergeant Webb, driving the last vehicle in line, used his car-to-car radio channel to keep the units in tight formation as they sped down Normandie Avenue.

With every nerve jumping, I watched the aerial news coverage. Everything seemed to be moving in slow motion as I continued humming the Phil Collins song to myself. The patrol units were getting closer to the flash point. Several news stations broadcast a view of the radio cars from the ground level. They covered the entire action from the front, side, and rear as they sped by, and from high above in the air.

A newscaster in one of the helicopters expressed disbelief upon witnessing this unusual formation. He then picked up in the distance the LASD Air unit thundering in. At the same time and from a distance another news copter behind the LASD Air unit picked up the radio cars and support helicopter sending goose bumps up my spine. When the lead patrol car neared the intersection of Florence and Normandie Avenues, pockets of billowing smoke could be seen in the air. Law enforcement engagement was finally occurring. The advancing sirens could be heard and people and vehicles loaded with stolen goods paused, then scattered in all directions.

With precision reminiscent of pilots of the famous United States Navy Blue Angels, the patrol units entered the intersection of Florence and Normandie Avenues, sirens screaming and red lights flashing. The vehicles opened up the tight single file formation to form a circle as one unit went left and the other right, one right after the other. Many of the looters and rioters in the streets scattered as viewers watching on television finally observed law enforcement engaging the unruly crowd.

Korean-American and other business owners raised their hands, cheering in triumph and appreciation, from behind barricades in their doorways to the rooftops of their businesses. Only moments before, they were innocent victims fighting for their lives and businesses.

After encircling the semi-truck and the downed Reginald Denny with their patrol cars, the helmeted deputies quickly exited their cars. One pre-designated group led by Sergeant Webb formed a rescue circle and moved in on Denny while the others took a position of safety behind their cars, drawing down with their shotguns and AR-15 assault rifles on the surrounding crowd who had begun to fall back.

In my mind I watched the action from the television feed provided by the news copter. I felt a powerful burst of energy, confident we would make the rescue and begin to control some of the worst disturbance— even as some rocks and bottles were being hurled at the deputies and radio cars.

The rescue team, battling the initial onslaught of flying debris, was able to reach the truck driver who lay unconscious, bleeding profusely from the head after the assailants ran off. The crowd in the surrounding area then became more aggressive, throwing even more rocks and bottles at the approaching deputies. The first two deputies were able to lift the moaning Denny—one by his shoulders, the other by his feet—and carry him back toward the circle of patrol cars while three others provided protection with batons, riot shields, and with weapons at the ready.

A field reporter for the *Los Angeles Times* snapped off shot after shot of the action and rescue attempt. Rocks and bottles continued to fly. Suddenly from a distance, a deep roar of thunder from the approaching air support was heard.

The LASD helicopter was quickly moving in at a very low altitude. Positioned on each of the side doors above the skids, SWAT team members wearing ballistic helmets hovered over the area. Each held an assault rifle, pointed down at the crowd as they circled and provided air support to those deputies involved in the ground activity below.

The game had now changed. Word spread that Los Angeles County Sheriff's deputies were there and many rioters in the remaining crowd dispersed in all directions. Those looting the nearby businesses scampered off with whatever they could carry.

After reaching one of the patrol cars, deputies shoved the bleeding Denny into the back seat. One deputy jumped into the back with Denny who was in obvious pain, applying pressure to his severe head wounds with a white towel emblazoned in blue letters with *LA County*. Sergeant Webb ordered another deputy behind the wheel. The patrol car rolled Code 3 southbound on Normandie Avenue out of the intersection and back to the nearby fire station where paramedics awaited, prepared to provide immediate treatment to Denny.

One of the news helicopters, monitoring the flight of the radio car, actually caught a glimpse of a gunshot fired into the radio car by an unknown assailant. The shot glanced off the front hood and shattered the windshield. Luckily it didn't penetrate or injure anyone, or disable the vehicle. The televised rescue ended with the rescuing radio car safely arriving at the fire station and Denny being treated and transferred to an ambulance for transport to the hospital.

This dramatic rescue caught, not only the attention of the rioting mob, but thousands of citizens as well who were watching television as they arrived home from work.

The LAPD command staff and officers were watching the televised rescue as well, some at the command post at 54th Street and Van Ness Avenue. This was approximately seventeen city blocks northwest of the flash point—close enough to act. As the deputies in the intersection gradually forced open their rescue circle of patrol cars to include the entire intersection, they gathered up additional assault victims, while the LASD helicopter continued circling above providing air support.

The crowd's sense of momentum shifted. They were no longer in control. The cops were there and they weren't leaving. The local citizenry knew one thing for sure—when the Sheriff's Department responded and got involved, things would be taken care of appropriately.

Seeing this forced the LAPD command staff to finally engage its field forces. Orders from the top of LAPD hit the command post, coming down like lightning bolts. In the distance, news helicopter cameras picked up a platoon of LAPD radio cars coming in from their northern command post in the distance. People at home, who might have been lured in to engage in the violence, began to have second thoughts about joining those who were still being televised looting and setting fires at other locations. Although disturbances and looting continued, the tide had changed as police engaged. Things were about to change in a drastic way. I knew I had made the right decision.

My mental flight ended abruptly.

Chapter 6

BACK TO REALITY

ergeant Weiss, did you hear me?"

I snapped out of my dream. I could feel sweat dripping down my forehead. The captain asked again. "Sergeant, did you hear me?"

I mumbled, "Yes, sir."

I wish I could describe the deep discouragement I felt hearing the captain's words. My entire life—everything I had worked toward—had prepared me for an experience, such as the riots. I knew what to do and how to do it, but I had deep respect for authority and the command structure. My training stood between me and the difference my plan could have made for thousands of people.

I couldn't override the captain's decision. I stood there numb. I knew without a doubt my plan would have had an impact. I also knew it would never come to pass. Although I came very close to disobeying his orders, I knew better, even with the circumstances as they were, with lives on the line.

I felt comfortable later being able to articulate to my superiors why I made the decision I did and why the plan would have worked. Perhaps that's what made it so difficult to stand down and watch the events of the week ahead. My diverse background, experiences in deadly force, encounters with armed suspects, and the various positions of leadership I held throughout my life, prepared me to make the decision to deploy.

I looked away from the captain and watched the television monitor. The captain turned around and went upstairs to his office. He was not seen by me again that evening.

While we had been talking, looters were swelling in large numbers at the intersection of Florence and Normandie. The crowd, mostly opportunists and criminals, broke into local businesses, smashing windows if necessary, cheering as they carried away merchandise. They grabbed small items, TVs—whatever they could carry and then fled.

The worst part was watching the children. Not only were adults committing crimes in front of their kids, but children were being encouraged to participate in the looting and destruction. I wonder how the riots impacted those impressionable minds. What would they have to say about the experience as adults, two-and-a-half decades later? How would they justify their actions to their own kids?

Fires were flaring up everywhere we looked. It was heartbreaking to watch while other merchants and citizens coming to the aid of store owners tried to put fires out with small pails of water. The effort was to no avail, as buildings—and lifelong dreams—burned to the ground.

Shortly after the captain issued his order to stand down we looked on as news cameras recorded a small group of African-American citizens—two men and two women—coming to the aid of Reginald Denny. One of those rescuers was a black man, Bobby Green Jr., a truck driver himself. He was at home near the intersection watching television when he saw the dying man lying in the street and rushed to the scene. Green transported Denny to Daniel Freeman Memorial Hospital in

Inglewood, where Denny underwent three hours of emergency brain surgery to remove two blood clots. It was a miracle he survived.

Later Bobby Green was asked about Denny's condition at the time he rescued him. "He was really, really, really, bad ... bad shape. He had big holes under his eyes. His head was busted ... everything. It looked like he was ready to go unconscious."

Two close friends of Denny's met him at the hospital and one on either side grabbed his hands and said, "Reggie we're here for you." A single tear rolled down Denny's cheek. There would be a long road of painful recovery ahead.

A week after Denny was beaten in front of the world, the television program, "Inside Edition" labeled the incident attempted murder. They located and interviewed another one of Denny's rescuers, T.J. Murphy.

The interviewer asked why he risked his own life to save Denny. Murphy answered, "A person is being beaten down ... a person needs help and he has no one to turn to ... and you're there—you have to feel pretty low if you don't offer your help."

Murphy and his girlfriend, Terri Barnett, who were on the scene with their young daughter, did more than offer Denny help. They, along with Bobbie Green Jr. and another person saved his life. By the time Murphy arrived, Reginald Denny, fighting for his life had miraculously struggled back into the cab of his truck while the mob moved on the other targets.

According to Murphy, there was already a young lady in the seat next to Denny attempting to help him. "His eyes were swollen. His head was enlarged from being beaten. I asked her how he was doing and she said, 'He's alive.'"

Reginald Denny is alive today because of those who could have remained in obscurity. Instead they braved the crowd and saved his life. Moments such as these remind people they aren't black or white—they are human.

At the same intersection, yet another violent assault was captured by the media. A newscaster was interviewing Mary Schmack from Daniel Freeman Hospital, the hospital Reginald Denny was taken to.

"*This afternoon,*" said Ms. Schmack, "*it was discussed at the hospitals that we should get ready to gear up because we could have busy evenings.*"

Male Newscaster: "*Are you working in conjunction with any of the other hospitals?*"

Mary Schmack: "*Not right now.*"

Male Newscaster: "*You can handle it, right?*"

Mary Schmack: "*Yes.*"

Female Newscaster: "*Mary, just give me an idea of what some of the injuries you're seeing are.*"

Mary Schmack: "*We're seeing people with cuts from broken glass all the way to people who have been severely beaten.*"

Female Newscaster: "*There are people of every color and every race … now this is one of the worst things we've seen all night.*"

The newscaster was talking about a Ford Bronco that was surrounded by an angry mob of about 30 people.

"*They dragged the driver out….*"

A Male Newscaster Interrupted dramatically: "*And beat him bloody. The poor guy never had a chance.*"

Female Newscaster: "*At one point somebody stepped in and helped him out of there.*"

A short time later, a breaking news report showed a couple of good Samaritans helping the injured Bronco driver. There was one person on each side of him forcing their way through the crowd to get him medical attention.

Male Newscaster: "*It's just bedlam down here and it's hard to sort out who is doing what.*"

The violence showed no sign of abating. Whites and Korean-Americans weren't the only victims. Fidel Lopez, a self-employed construction worker and Guatemalan immigrant, was ripped from his truck and robbed of nearly $2,000. Damian Williams smashed his forehead open with a car stereo as another rioter attempted to slice off his ear.

After Lopez lost consciousness, one of the attackers spray painted his chest, torso, and genitals with black paint. Reverend Bennie Newton, an African American minister who ran an inner-city ministry for troubled youth, prevented others from beating Lopez by placing himself between Lopez and his attackers and shouting, "Kill him and you have to kill me too."

Reverend Newton was instrumental in helping Lopez get critical medical aid by taking him to a hospital. Eight-days after he was savagely beaten and yanked from his truck, 47-year-old Fidel Lopez met his guardian angel in person—the man who had saved his life. Lopez's face was swollen from the 29 stitches in his forehead caused by a blow from the auto stereo. He had 17 stitches in the ear someone tried to slice off and 12 stitches under his chin. Lopez and the 59-year-old minister, who placed his body on top of him to protect him, hugged and cried.

"I passed through a bad moment," Lopez said to the brave and compassionate minister. "I thank you. You saved me."

Though Lopez sustained no broken bones, his body ached from blows to his back and shoulder. For some time, the pain in his head was unceasing.

In a few short hours, LAPD dispatchers took unending reports and calls of violence and request for assistance needed by several passing motorists. But the calls and requests were met with silence on the radio.

No LAPD officers responded. Not one.

Wednesday, 6:55 PM

Watching replays of the attacks from earlier in the day, I thought a lot that evening about why I had decided on a career in law enforcement.

Challenges aside, law enforcement is rewarding work. My father was a deputy and I lived law enforcement from a young age. Growing up I knew local deputies and went on ride-alongs with my dad. I was intrigued by the work. A lot of gratification comes from solving crimes and catching bad people. It's exciting work and it is satisfying when you can solve a crime.

When I was around 13 or 14-years-old, I went on a patrol ride along with my dad at the old Montrose Station, in an area that is now covered by the Crescenta Valley Station. An incident occurred which marked me.

We rolled Code 3 to a disturbance call. A former pro wrestler was under the influence of drugs, threatening people in a residential area, and using physical force on some. My father is only 5-10" tall and was about 170 lbs. at that time. He and his partner, of similar build, engaged this crazed individual in the street as other patrol units were responding.

The suspect was the size of Hulk Hogan. He attempted to rip the opened passenger side door off of the patrol car, when I caught his attention. I was sitting in the dark, in the back seat of the patrol car behind a metal screen with the rear doors closed. He verbally lashed out at me and I huddled there scared for myself and for my dad and his partner.

When other responding units arrived, a black deputy the same size as my dad, and a good friend of my dad, walked up to the suspect. Calmly he talked him down, bringing him under control. In his favor, this deputy had some previous encounters and dealings with the suspect. Later I learned that the suspect, after getting high on drugs, developed a fear of black people. The intimidation factor was successful in diffusing this incident. Talking worked when deadly force could have been necessary if the situation escalated.

The experience taught me a lot about the value of talking respectfully to people, controlling a situation, and planning ahead. It was also a good example of how quickly an incident can turn for the worse.

Now I had to communicate the captain's decision whether I believed in it or not. Disheartened and frustrated, I walked up to the station desk personnel. "We will not be sending our response team anywhere outside of our station patrol area. Tell everyone to stand down and stay in our jurisdictional areas, per the captain's orders."

"Have Sergeant Webb set up a large command post across the street from the fire station." This was our initial staging area, at Washington High School. "Contact Lost Hills, Marina Del Rey, Carson, and West Hollywood and tell them to put their emergency response personnel on standby in case I need them to respond to our station area later."

I felt sick inside. My gut feeling told me that it wouldn't be long before we would be completely inundated and forced to deal with escalating problems in our own area, since LAPD was not taking any action and we could not intervene. Even though the flash point of the disturbances was a very short distance away, it was out of our jurisdiction. The captain had taken any ability to respond out of our hands.

"Contact the Inmate Reception Center (IRC) and activate an emergency field booking team," I added. "Have them prepare a semi-truck trailer and mass booking team personnel. Get some buses ready and send everything along with extra booking equipment to our command post at Washington High School."

Wednesday, 7:05 PM

Emergency phone calls were pouring in to the station desk personnel at an alarming rate. Although a peaceful rally of 2,000 people was underway at the nearby First African Methodist Episcopal Church, looting and rioting began in earnest in several areas, including the adjacent city of Inglewood.

Witnesses and victims passing by in vehicles or walking the streets in our jurisdictional areas on Normandie Avenue, Century Boulevard, and Vermont Avenue, flooded the dispatch center with robbery, assault, burglary, and fire calls.

The news media continued its play-by-play sensationalist coverage.

"We heard the 911 circuits are overloaded this evening by people calling with isolated small incidents…".

"Along the Harbor freeway, police are advising motorists to stay off these off ramps … to stay out of the area because as you can see you don't know what's going to happen. People are getting hurt."

Fires, beatings and destruction—it seemed no one was going to be exempt from the mayhem and devastation that night.

Twenty three years after the riots I discovered by accident that a man I had known for years not only had a front row seat to the ruin, but lived to tell about it. Young Chul, owner of a small convenience store, witnessed but was not a victim of the riot going on right outside the front door of his convenience store in South Central. His was the only business left standing, unscathed, as others were destroyed and burned to the ground around him. The relationships he built in the neighborhood over the years were his saving grace. As it turned out, the mutual respect he had fostered with customers shielded Young Chul from the destruction so many suffered.

Wednesday, 7:15 PM

My fears were real. A tsunami wave of disturbances from LAPD's South Central 77th Division crashed down on our northern boundary area. I turned to Deputy Everett, my watch deputy.

"Call our early morning personnel in early. Advise them of what's going on and let them know they might have problems getting in to work."

"Yes, sir."

"All PM personnel are to remain on duty past their regular hours until advised otherwise."

I sounded a little rough, so I turned and added with a smile, "Looks like it's going to be a long night."

"Yes, sir, it does." Everett smiled back.

LAPD's non-response, supposedly maintaining a strong visible presence without making arrests, escalated the worsening situation. Looters and arsonists grew ever bolder under the eyes of the watching police who did nothing to stop them. A violent firestorm of chaos was allowed to grow unchecked. LAPD was worried about tying up their resources. This, coupled with poor planning, and an inadequate communications system, turned out to be a fatal tactical mistake.

Live TV news footage showed police parked in their radio cars failing to respond to the jeering taunts of the rioters. LAPD cars also drove by slowly, watching as looters broke store windows and filled their vehicles with stolen goods.

A Channel 7 newscaster questioned the helicopter reporter:

"That's a structure fire, isn't it Ron?"

"It's actually a storefront, Paul. We're going to move in closer."

As the camera honed in on the burning building, two fire trucks and an EMT vehicle pulled up to the fire. About a block away, the camera focused on five police cars. Emergency bar lights spinning, they appeared to be creating a barrier to block the street.

"The police and firefighters are in extreme danger tonight and our hats are off to them. We appreciate all they are doing."

Newscaster Ann: *"And we're working on a map to show you the spots around Los Angeles you want to keep your family away from tonight. If you're going to head out to church, you should know the First American Methodist Church is packed to the gills. They're coalescing there to discuss the issues of the day and to share their thoughts and feelings and their anger mainly."*

∿

Fire officials raged with frustration about the inadequate police response. Rioters turned on fire fighters trying to extinguish fires. It was dangerous to go in unescorted. At one point, more than 30 structural fires raged while an estimated 20 fire engines idled, waiting for police escorts, who also sat idle waiting for orders.

Yet the LA City Fire Department did eventually respond to fires for hours that evening--without police escort in a mob-controlled city. They were committed. During the first few hours at least a dozen attempts to kill firefighters were documented. Still, they refused to stand by while the city burned. Firefighters worked diligently, even though their personal safety was at risk. One firefighter, Scott Miller, was shot in the face as he drove a fire truck toward a blaze.

As the evening wore on, the fire department used a "hit and run" approach, dousing fires as best as possible and moving on. LAPD was overwhelmed by the rapid and widespread arson and unprepared to respond. So overwhelmed in fact they could not provide timely or accurate information to the media, who was demanding to know what was going on and what they were doing.

Four hours in, the game was on. The score: LAPD-0. The rioters had the advantage and they were leading by a significant distance. Things were already out of hand and something had to be done quickly. Governor Wilson announced his dissatisfaction over the unwillingness and or inability of LAPD to retake the streets of South Central to protect area residents.

Wednesday, 7:25 PM

I was inundated with a continuous wave of phone calls from departmental executives looking for answers. I would no sooner end one call than somebody else was calling. Under Sheriff Bob Edmonds, Assistant Sheriff Jerry Harper and Commander Mark Squiers demanded to know what we were doing at Lennox Station, noting we were so close to the flash point.

During a lighter moment in one of those tense conversations, Assistant Sheriff Jerry Harper told me not to be afraid to open the check book and spend his money. I laughed and told him that I had already written a few checks and spent a huge chunk of the balance. I had ordered the IRC booking team out and called for the activation of the Field Operations Region II, which included all nearby stations. This would be an expensive operation for LASD all across the city.

I informed him that I had requested all personnel in the region to be ordered on 12-on and 12-off shifts. I told him I called in the early morning shift personnel early, as well as holding all PM personnel over. He gave me a big chuckle and lots of encouragement in grappling with the tough decisions we were faced with at the time. We were in no way making light of the situation, but it helped to relieve the tension.

Frantic citizens continued their barrage of calls into the station asking for help. Intelligence reports came in from area field units listing major assaults and robberies throughout South Central and spilling into surrounding areas. Looters were running into stores even as fires burned within. Burning buildings toppled into the streets creating hazards and tying up traffic. Worse though, were reports and live news coverage of civilian assaults.

The world looked on while the city burned and innocent people died.

Wednesday, 8:15 PM

As LAPD Chief Daryl Gates much later acknowledged, LAPD committed a major tactical blunder during the first hours of unrest, as no police were around to help. A nation watched on television as news helicopters hovered overhead. Presumably Gates saw it as well.

Refraining from engaging the crowd and going in to rescue Reginald Denny, Chief Gates was later quoted as saying, "You cannot respond softly to a riot, you must move in and move in quickly. If we had it to do over, we would have used deadly weapons to get into that intersection."

Ironic words, I thought when I heard this.

Gates himself, in his own words, had only affirmed that my proposed plan to rescue Denny, which the Captain had forbidden, was the logical, humane, and correct response.

Wednesday, 8:30 PM

Havoc continued throughout the evening, the rioters striking in new territories and taking out their anger on unguarded businesses. Once the intersection of Florence and Normandie was completely looted, burned, and destroyed, the mindless rioters moved into other South Central neighborhoods. Mayor Tom Bradley called a local state of emergency. Moments later, Gov. Pete Wilson, at Bradley's request, ordered the National Guard to activate 2,000 reserve soldiers.

At this time some LAPD patrol units were spotted in the area of the Florence and Normandie intersection lighting flares and directing traffic. Too little, and way too late. Looters threw bricks and stones to smash windows and Molotov cocktails—homemade bottle-based weapons— to start fires. Once they realized LAPD would do nothing the madness swept on. The LAPD presence didn't seem to deter the violence. Cars were torched to block intersections. Others were carjacked as nameless, faceless and hapless drivers who stumbled into the scene were beaten and cast mercilessly aside. Numerous shots were fired at rescue personnel. The more the violence escalated, the harsher our efforts to restore peace would have to be. I didn't like this thought. People were going to be hurt, including our deputies, looters, arsonists, and bystanders as well.

Wednesday, 9:40 PM

I was relieved as watch commander by the station's Operations Lieutenant, Tony Denis, whom I thought highly of and was glad to see. I stayed on as his backup throughout the night. We worked shoulder-to-shoulder to maintain the continuity of the strategy I had initiated earlier. I also assisted him when new missions and problems arose. We worked flat-out hour-after-hour. Phones rang continuously. Instead of improving, the situation only seemed to worsen.

Female News Anchor: *"There are about eight fires going on right now. We saw earlier one about three doors down from Tom's Liquor Store. About an hour ago, we saw fire trucks being escorted by police officers. Up until then we saw no police presence. That could be for any number of reasons. They may have pulled out of the area hoping not to make the situation more volatile."*

Male News Anchor: *"We have an advisory from the city. Police are asking us to inform police officers that the entire department has been placed on tactical alert status and it's because of the sporadic violence in the wake of today's verdicts."*

He repeated an earlier advisory, *"LA City Fire department also advises that all fire chiefs are being asked to report to work."*

A countywide departmental tactical alert had been called for by an executive, keeping all sworn departmental personnel on 12 hour shifts. All officers on duty were to remain on duty. All days off were cancelled. Some off-duty officers were asked to report in for duty. Area updates were provided to the Emergency Operations Bureau (EOB) as a flurry of activity developed throughout the night.

Wednesday, 10:00 PM

Looters had set off a chain reaction as greed-inflamed opportunities to grab and snatch from unprotected storefronts. Why not? The police weren't there to stop them. Everybody wanted theirs. Get it now. It didn't matter what they had to do to get it; risk fires, risk cuts from broken windows. There was no consequence to grabbing whatever was available and dragging it home. Watching this rampage of theft and destruction, I'm sure I was not the only one wondering why people would destroy their own neighborhoods and the businesses they depended on in their daily life. They obviously weren't in their right minds. This was unthinking, primal and hysterical mob behavior.

LAPD gradually moved in over the evening, but agonizingly slowly. Fire Fighters were still under attack. Members of LAPD Metropolitan B and C platoons were involved in a firefight at 114th Street and Central Avenue while protecting Fire Department personnel. They fired hundreds of rounds and sent in their V-100 rescue vehicle to safely extract the officers. Gunfire continued to pierce the sky. Buildings burned and adjacent palm trees caught fire, blazing up like Tiki torches. Innocent people caught up in the madness were beaten bloody. Others died in pain as ambulances could not get through.

School districts, bus service, and other community services were affected by the violence and as evening progressed, numerous shutdowns were ordered in the South Central Los Angeles area. Los Angeles City Mayor Tom Bradley called for a local state of emergency.

A demonstration outside of Parker Center, LAPD's headquarters, started to turn violent after 9 PM as the crowd threw rocks, smashed windows, and torched a parking lot kiosk. Other demonstrators vandalized several downtown buildings and traffic on city streets and the Hollywood Freeway 101 was soon impacted. The California Highway Patrol closed exit ramps from the Harbor Freeway 110, from the Santa Monica Freeway 10 junction to Century Boulevard to keep unsuspecting motorists from wandering into the path of violence. Eventually the closure was moved south, stretching from Martin Luther King Boulevard to Imperial Highway.

"Along the Harbor freeway, Police are advising motorists to stay off these off ramps … to stay out of the area because as you can see you don't

know what' going to happen. People are getting hurt. We have an advisory from the city. Police are asking us to inform police officers that the entire department has been placed on tactical alert status and it's because of the sporadic violence in the wake of today's verdicts. LA City Fire also advises that all fire chiefs are being asked to report to work."

The boundaries of the riots widened. A police helicopter had been fired upon. After LAPD notified the Federal Aviation Administration (FAA) of this development they shifted the landing pattern of jetliners approaching the Los Angeles International Airport for safety reasons. Anyone planning a trip to Los Angeles or connecting with other flights through LAX was now being affected.

Not everyone who was upset about the verdicts chose to react with violence. There were also peaceful demonstrations taking place around the city. About 200-300 demonstrators gathered at the Hansen Dam Recreation Center in Lake View Terrace, near the site of the initial traffic stop and beating of Rodney King, and marched to the nearby LAPD Foothill Division station headquarters.

Wednesday, 11:00 PM

Mayor Bradley issued a taped message to the citizens of Los Angeles calling for peace. Over the next few hours support began arriving as several assisting sheriff's patrol units from various stations arrived at our command post. Some were also diverted south to Carson Station.

Wednesday, 11:50 PM

The number and intensity of fires continued to increase, especially in the northern Vermont District along 106th Street, Budlong Avenue, 98th Street, and in the Vermont Avenue areas. Reports of 35-40 people arrested, solely in our sheriff's jurisdictional area of Lennox, began to filter in. It was good to know that at least our guys were being proactive.

Midnight

Governor Wilson held a news conference announcing a state of emergency and that he was dispatching additional National Guard and California Highway Patrol. The U.S. military was placed on alert.

In between breaking stories, the media replayed events televised throughout the afternoon and evening. On one hand, it gave both citizens and law enforcement a bird's eye view of what was going down; on the other hand, that continuous excited coverage may have contributed significantly to the mounting destruction. Earlier in the day, African-American City councilmember (1987-2002) Nate Holden blamed the media for the violence, saying; "When are you going to assume your responsibility as well … you hyped this thing all the way to D-Day."

Thursday, April 30th, 12:15 AM

The numbers of deployed personnel increased despite a city/county-wide curfew implemented by Mayor Bradley. Reports came in of shots being fired at an Inglewood Police Department car. By midnight at least eight deaths had been reported and more than two dozen injuries were attributed to the initial stages of the riot. What did it accomplish? Who did it serve?

~

Reports flowed in from around the country.

News anchor:

"The fuse in the Rodney King case was lit in Los Angeles but it stretched all across America. In Atlanta, a reported 300 arrests were made by police and Atlanta Mayor Maynard Jackson has issued orders that a curfew would be in effect this evening from 11pm until 5am.

Around the country people are angry … demonstrating in the first few hours after the acquittal in California."

Disturbing video was broadcasted even from the Midwest where people who were angry about the verdicts also committed crimes. Somebody broke into a police department in Wisconsin and damaged three dozen police cars. The vandal(s) left a note linking the destruction to the Rodney King verdicts. People were angry, and not just African-Americans. I had to wonder how much of the fury was fueled by the waves of sensationalized media coverage and how much was actually a release of frustration.

In New York City the bells of Saint John the Divine Catholic Church rang to celebrate what church officials called "solidarity with the people of Los Angeles." A New York City councilmember whose father represented Harlem in Congress was videoed standing next to Rev. Al Sharpton and said angrily, "It makes you hate this country, the United States of America. It makes you hate America," and pointing to the flag he said, "It makes you hate that flag. It makes you hate cops and it makes you hate all white people. Who can even begin to think you can excuse this verdict?"

Harsh words—actually, bordering on treason. What did they mean? What did America and our flag have to do with a verdict rendered by 12 people? It was because of the flag he cursed that this councilman had the right to say those words without fear of legal retribution.

No, Los Angeles would not be suffering alone the first night of the riots. By the time night turned in to early morning hours the city smelled scorched. A rain of ash fell from the skies. Resources already strained by fires from the day before, the Los Angeles Fire Department was overwhelmed. New fires were being reported by the minute.

Thursday, 6:30 AM

I was relieved by the dayshift supervisory personnel after a seventeen-hour shift and ordered to go home. I was to report in again at 6 PM that night for my twelve-hour shift. I briefed the oncoming supervisors on the past day and evening's events in the watch commander's office. The logs showed page after page of horrific violence. Doubtless, they'd probably also been glued to the television. They already knew the LAPD had gone MIA.

I thought about Captain Monroe's lack of leadership and courage. I was frustrated and tried to come to terms with his reasoning. Captain Monroe had many testaments of success throughout his long career and this decision made no sense.

Leadership positions within law enforcement are sometimes the most stressful and demanding and not everyone is right for the job. Experience provides for some of the training, yet some people are best at being support staff while others are born leaders. I have found those who have really earned their position of leadership, with a well-rounded body of experience of many years, often times with an advanced education, and who are balanced and grounded individuals, make for the best leaders in law enforcement.

One can speculate as to how things might have turned out had Captain Monroe allowed the execution of my plan, but one thing was for sure—they would have been different. At the dawning of the second day, everyone in that room knew we had missed a golden opportunity.

Chapter 7

THE RIDE
HOME AND BACK

fter the meeting, I changed clothes in the locker room and walked out to my car. I pulled out of the station driveway as daylight approached and drove toward Hawthorne Boulevard on my way to Century Boulevard and to the northbound 405 freeway. I saw clouds of smoke to the north and east of the station engulfing the South Central Los Angeles area. I shook my head feeling this couldn't be real.

I felt a surge of anger and helplessness. Driving northbound on the 405 freeway, the events of the long afternoon and night overwhelmed me. I listened to the car radio for the updated riot news: death, destruction, and assaults—all for what?

I felt like a total failure, knowing that if I'd been able to implement my plan, I could have changed the direction of the night's events and ultimately the history of that terrible week. The opportunity to stop the madness had slipped away in seconds. I was obsessed with the thought.

City officials were concerned about how to put a curfew in place and enforce it in a city as large as Los Angeles. LA covers a lot of ground as the second largest city in the U.S., lying in a large coastal basin surrounded on three sides by mountains reaching up to and over 10,000 feet, it comprises just short of 469 square miles—extending 44 miles longitudinally and 29 miles latitudinal.

A citywide curfew would have been difficult enough to enforce, but this riot had spread beyond the limits of the City of Los Angeles. It bled out of city boundaries into unincorporated areas of LA County. City officials knew very well that even with a curfew in place, people could just get into their cars and drive to an area where there were no police and start more trouble.

Newscaster Dan Blackburn Reported:

"This is a city where last night when the trouble began, people spoke of it as a reaction to the Rodney King verdict. That may have been true then, it is doubtful that it is true now. Indeed, what is taking place in this city at this moment borders on insurrection as rioting, looting and arson has hopscotched across the city."

I made it home in time to see my son off to school, and my wife to work, and reassure them I was okay. My wife had been worried, knowing I was in the eye of the storm. As I watched her pull out of the driveway, I thought about people whose lives changed drastically over the prior 18 hours. Those who lost homes or businesses, or in some cases, been injured or had someone close die. Many people would never again have the opportunity to say hello or good-bye to a child, or console a parent, or loved one.

I thought about those who had lost their lives in the hours before and also about those who had to inform families of a loved one's passing. I knew firsthand how hard that was. The most difficult thing I ever had to do was to deliver a death notification to a girl in her twenties in the middle of the night. Her brother had taken a rifle to his head and committed suicide. That is one thing I will never forget.

I saw a lot of death in my career, but losses of innocent life were hard to come to terms with. This riot would see many before it was over. Both civilians and law enforcement would suffer with indelible memories that would undoubtedly resurface throughout their lives.

An incident that occurred in 1984 really hit home for me and after everything I've seen and done, it's still with me. I responded to a call for an assault with a deadly weapon taking place between a couple of Hispanics and a valet parking attendant on Melrose Avenue in West Hollywood. After an argument the suspects left and then a while later came back—this time armed. They chased the parking attendant down the sidewalk as he tried to get into the front door of the restaurant. They caught up to him and shot him from behind, point-blank with a shotgun.

I arrived within 30 seconds of the call. The suspects had already gotten into their car and were probably headed southbound. I approached the victim, who was on the sidewalk at the front door. His back was steaming hot with all of the pellet rounds that had entered his body. He was dead before I arrived. I have never forgotten the memory of that incident.

Incidents of death and destruction were rising over the last 18 hours. Lives changed drastically. I thought about the merchants who lost everything they owned. Their businesses burned to the ground in front of them as they waited for police who would never arrive. They were powerless to intervene as a lifetime of hard work was reduced to ash. Others were forced to stand by helplessly and watch thieves carry away armloads of their livelihood. This was no exaggeration. We saw it happen.

Luckily, I lived in an area that was virtually free of any chaos or disturbances. I wondered, in light of the television coverage of what in most instances were racially motivated attacks, how many people would look at their neighbors differently today. Would there be judgment where there was once acceptance? Hatred where there was friendship? There is often a thin line between polarities—good and bad, hot and cold. Today the division between black and white was more distinct than it had been for decades. Over the years, many lives had been given in the forging of bonds between the races only to watch bridges burned in a matter of hours during the riots.

~

Any kind of decent daytime sleep is tough enough to get under normal circumstances, but I was so amped up that my sleepless day felt longer than the riot-filled night I had just lived through. I couldn't shut my mind off. Flash-frame pictures of what I had seen kept me awake. I dozed off here and there but a restful sleep eluded me until I finally fell asleep in the afternoon, just in time to get up and get ready to go back to work. I showered and then ate dinner turning on the television to see what was happening. I had hoped I would wake up to reports that rioting had subsided and things were under control. To the contrary, the disturbances had spread significantly.

News reporters were saying there was talk about bringing in the US Army.

"This is a situation that, as far as we can tell, authorities are unable to control."

The State of Emergency declared the night before made way for the National Guard. Troops had responded to their area armories and began deploying in earnest. Later in the day I learned that they were delayed taking refresher courses and waiting for equipment, ammunition, and deployment orders. By late afternoon they were finally deployed to hot spots throughout the South Central Los Angeles area.

Violence still appeared widespread and unchecked as heavy looting and fires intensified throughout Los Angeles County. Because it appeared LAPD had abandoned Koreatown, The Korean-American community organized armed security teams comprised of store owners and employees to defend their livelihoods from assault by the ruthless mobs of armed looters.

Korean-language radio stations called for volunteers to help Korean-American merchants guarding against rioters. Korean immigrants from the area rushed to Koreatown to help. Open gun battles were televised between rioters, store owners and their defenders. Many were armed with a variety of improvised weapons, shotguns, and semi-automatic rifles. This kind of armory in the hands of untrained civilians was a dangerous situation. Nonetheless, Korean-American shopkeepers were forced to shoot at the mobs to protect their businesses—and most likely their lives—from large crowds of violent looters. Jay Rhee, a storeowner in the area, stated to The Los Angeles Times: "We have lost faith in the police." Rhee and the Korean-American community were not alone in this feeling.

Organized law enforcement response finally began to come together by mid-day on Thursday. Fire crews began to respond, backed by police escorts, many of them CHP reinforcements airlifted into the city.

Watching the fires, I was hoping there were no people in the burning buildings. Did the arsonists bother to check before they struck their matches? Years before, I was called to a fire in a three story hotel structure on Sunset Strip. People were jumping out of their windows when I got there. It's hard to forget trying to save people while they're burning or desperately trying to survive.

Mayor Bradley, along with Los Angeles City Fire Chief Donald Manning and Los Angeles City Police Chief Daryl Gates, held a news conference on the violence rocking the city. By mid-afternoon the United States Attorney General, William Barr, announced that the Justice Department would resume its investigation into possible civil rights violations in the King beating. Governor Wilson held a news conference urging an end to the violence and promising sufficient law enforcement resources to bring the violence and havoc under control. Despite the expansion of city and county curfews, a Department of Motor Vehicles (DMV) office was burned to the ground in Long Beach.

The day ahead was filled with looting of retail outlets in South Central LA, Koreatown, Hollywood, Mid-Wilshire, Watts, Westwood, Beverly Hills, Compton, Culver City, Hawthorne, Long Beach, Norwalk, and Pomona. There was no indication that the rioting would end soon. Panic took over much of the city. Long lines formed at supermarkets and gas stations throughout the city as residents, fearing shortages, stocked up. Many South Central supermarket shelves were bare by evening.

The riots weren't even close to being over. Public safety became a countywide focus as government offices, courthouses, and libraries closed. Fearing that looting and vandalism might spread more, shopping malls and businesses shut down for the day.

Some colleges closed for the day and final exams were cancelled at others. The entire Los Angeles Unified School District closed all of its schools and child care centers. Mail service was suspended in 14 zip codes. Local professional sports teams, the Los Angeles Dodgers and Los Angeles Clippers, cancelled their home games.

Thursday, 4:30 PM

As I drove my Chevy pickup truck onto the freeway south into work late Thursday afternoon I listened to radio reports describing the chaos that was now my life.

Newscaster: *"Preliminary reports indicate at least 25 deaths since the verdicts were announced yesterday afternoon, acquitting four police officers involved in the beating of Rodney King on March 3, 1991, There have been more than 500 injuries and 1,000 fires, resulting in over 700 arrests. Property damage is estimated at over $200 million dollars."*

It was incredible to think that all of this occurred in less than 24 hours, from the initial stages and turning point, to the moment I could have altered this madness with my strategy to some degree. Each fire, every reported loss of life and property, stung. I wished I could go back in time to launch my plan and avert the destruction. It would have been easier if the time between my giving the go-ahead and my Captain's crushing decision to "stand down" had been distanced by more than a few minutes. But there was no going back.

I began humming and whispering the lyrics to another one of my favorite songs by Phil Collins, "Another Day in Paradise," and one by John Secada , "Just Another Day," as I flashed back to the highlights of the day before.

I drove over the Mulholland pass on the southbound 405 freeway. Huge plumes of smoke billowed up across the city as helicopters flew through acrid smoke along the horizon. The city was on fire. The smoke covered the sky with an opaque, yellow tinge. I looked up to find the sun and all I could see behind the veil of smoke was a bright spot surrounded by a halo of light. I rolled my window down about three inches to let in some air. A pungent stench filled the truck. It smelled like burning wood or smoke from a bonfire, but at the same time there was an underlying odor—sharp and unpleasant—the scent of burning chemicals.

I felt like I was entering a war zone. The fact of the matter being—I was.

I exited the freeway at La Cienega Boulevard and Century Boulevard near LAX, encountering a huge crowd of looters in the street as I rounded the corner and passed under the freeway overpass onto Century Boulevard at Felton Avenue. Several of the mom and pop and chain stores, including a laundromat, had been destroyed and were burning. Ash, carried by the breeze, fell from the sky. Debris was scattered everywhere. It seemed as though I was driving onto a movie set.

Looters pushed shopping carts loaded with merchandise including such simple things as diapers and toilet paper. Ordinary people caught up in the hysteria, were taking the opportunity to steal necessities. As I approached, individuals in the crowd moved suddenly into the street in front of me to block my path. I reached across to the passenger seat next to me and opened my fanny pack. Pulling out my Beretta 9MM pistol, I held it in my right hand and placed an extra magazine clip between my legs.

The crowd was diverse, made up of both young and old. Many held stolen merchandise or other objects. Dusk was setting in and I was unable to tell exactly what they were carrying. Possibly weapons, I thought.

I scanned the immediate area. There were no avenues of escape. Some of the vehicles behind me stopped, blocking my ability to back up or turn around. This was going to be ugly.

The only side street near me was short and would lead me into a hostile gang neighborhood paralleling the freeway and abutting some of the burned-out businesses. I flashed back to the images on the news programs the day before, as drivers were pulled from their cars and savagely beaten.

There was only one option.

Breathing deeply, showing no fear, I moved my pickup truck slowly toward the crowd. I steered with my left hand down low, placing my right hand high on the steering wheel and holding my loaded and cocked Beretta, making it very obvious I was armed.

As I neared the crowd a heavy-set, tattooed, Hispanic man at the front of the group jeered at me, almost as if he recognized me, and motioned with his hands for the hostile and angry crowd to back away allowing me to pass through. Several people yelled obscenities as I slowly drove by. I could feel the tension and hostility of the crowd as several plastic water bottles struck my windshield and other parts of my truck.

I took another deep breath safely passing the crowd. I had been mentally prepared to drive through the raging mass and fire my weapon if necessary—both of which were the last things I wanted to do. But there was no way I going down like Reginald Denny had the day before. No one was going to pull me into the street and rob and beat me.

I was still feeling the surge of adrenaline as I drove the few remaining miles to the station. I was fully aware that I was lucky to have avoided a possible use of deadly force against this unruly crowd—especially if they had decided to rush the truck.

I drove southbound on Hawthorne Boulevard. I was saddened seeing many burned-out businesses along the way. Nearing Lennox Boulevard I prepared to turn left at the intersection and into the Lennox Sheriff's Station driveway near the corner. I paused. I could not believe what I saw.

The Payless Shoe Store, directly across the street from and diagonally adjacent to the station, was on fire. I couldn't believe what I was seeing. We went from holding our own area in check the day before to losing a business right across the street from the sheriff's station. I felt as if I was living in a movie. This must be a movie. None of it seemed real.

The absolute devastation reminded me of photos I had seen of war-torn regions in third world countries. I could not believe it happened in the city I worked in. I could not understand the senselessness of it all. Had I been given a chance, I could have stopped it from happening in this senseless way.

We could have done something to change this.

I live with that guilt to this day.

Chapter 8
DAY TWO
AND BEYOND

Thursday, 6:00 PM

The station was backlogged with a number of old calls for service from hours before, so we were generally in a reactionary mode trying to catch up. We chased the radio all night responding to one serious, adrenaline-soaked situation after another. Fires, stabbings, shots-fired calls, looting and assault calls dominated the night and were of course our priorities. Protecting fire crews was also a priority. Shots were still being taken at many of the fire fighters. The Rapid Transit District (RTD) suspended all bus service, effective at 6 PM which quieted the evening somewhat.

We were short of radio cars with the station placed on 12 hours on and 12 hours off shifts, so I was assigned as driver of a four-man car. Another sergeant and two deputies were with me as partners for the long evening and early morning. Because of the unpredictable nature of violent uprisings, and for safety and tactical reasons, it was imperative to have personnel grouped together in numbers as much as possible.

Although riot-related crimes were our focus that night, deputies on street patrol must always be ready to take action. Even in an area where certain things go down on a regular basis, you have to be prepared for the unexpected. You can never predict exactly what's going to happen next. I learned this very early in my career, even before I was assigned to Lennox Station.

On October 15, 1985, I was involved in a shooting on the Sunset Strip, the mile-and-a-half stretch of Sunset Boulevard passing through West Hollywood. With its trademark array of massive billboards the Strip is a popular destination for tourists and locals alike. Something is always going on.

I was a training officer at the time and had a trainee with me on the early morning shift 11 PM-7 AM. It was fire season so first responders were all very busy.

A call came in to the station around 12:50 AM about a guy looking into cars in the parking lot behind Carlos and Charlies, a popular restaurant and nightclub hotspot on Sunset Boulevard. I said to the trainee, "I'll show you how you can help the other guys out even though it's not our call."

We ended up arriving as the first patrol unit on scene. The suspect was described as dressed all in white and said to be looking into cars in the back parking lot. We pulled up to the west side of the restaurant with the intention of pulling around to the back of the restaurant to see what was going on, but as we were on Sunset Blvd., things would change radically.

"There's a guy walking backwards out the front door holding a chrome handgun with a bunch of people around him," I said to my partner. He didn't see the suspect, who was holding the chrome revolver at eye level.

"He's definitely got a revolver," I said, "and it looks like he's holding a money bag in his left hand. There might be a robbery going down."

I got out of the car and ran taking a kneeling position behind a Mercedes Benz, parked on the sidewalk and in the circular driveway. The suspect continued walking backwards from the front door and into the circular driveway and continued pointing his weapon at several people. As if he knew exactly where I was, he quickly turned around and pointed his weapon at me as I yelled out, "Freeze, police!" I fired twice and I hit him from a distance of 30 feet.

Suddenly, the guy took off running to his left with only the right side of his body visible to me, still pointing his gun at me with his right arm fully extended. I fired two more shots striking him again and he fell down between another parked car and into a dirt planter area next to several tall juniper trees.

The interesting story is the guy didn't actually rob the place. A 37-year-old Hispanic, with a rap sheet a mile long, he got into an argument with someone inside as he was trying to pick up on his girlfriend and wanted to show himself as a big man when he was confronted. When we got over to him, the hammer was cocked back, but the gun, which was soon found not to be loaded, was lying under his body in a pool of blood and dirt.

The bag indeed was a Bank of America type money bag he had used to carry his weapon. Amazingly, he had a blood alcohol level of .33, which is dangerously high.

It was a big night at the restaurant. Eric Dickerson, a famous Los Angeles Rams football player at the time, had taken his offensive line to dinner and the place was packed. Even though the caper went down at 12:50 AM, there were a lot of witnesses. Several people were standing outside waiting for their vehicles from the valet parkers. It was a pretty traumatic experience for many—including myself. I was only 27 years old.

~

Toward the end of the long and trying night, my partners and I were ready to head back to the station. Before we did, I slowly drove into a strip mall and through the parking lot without headlights on. Each of us peered into the darkness, trying to spot looters or arsonists. Every shadow held some kind of threat.

Suddenly we heard a loud thud under the vehicle. We all gasped.

"What the heck was that?" one of my partners asked.

"I'm not sure." I tried to figure out what I struck. The object pushed the right side of the radio car into the air for what felt like a few feet.

Somebody said, "It feels like we just ran over a body."

This was hardly out of the realm of possibility on a night like this. Fearing the worst, I stopped the car and we exited the vehicle, quickly glancing around the area and rooftops, seeking cover.

I said softly, "Look for snipers! Let's make sure we're not being set up for an ambush."

The parking lot was pitch black and eerily silent. Just as in every other parking lot in the area, debris from the riots littered the area around the car. I shone my flashlight around, poking under some trash and weeds.

I yelled out, "Guys, we just hit a truck tire and rim."

The tension snapped and suddenly it was funny. We joked around, slapping each other on the back, playing the incident over again and again. We needed that laugh badly. It was the first break in the stress all night. Then we got serious again getting back into the car and listening to the chatter of the radio.

We headed to the station, the exhausting 12-hour shift almost over. The night had been good for me. I was thankful for the chance to get out into the field with the patrol crews and away from the watch commander's office and duties. I couldn't face the hour-and-a-half drive home. I was absolutely mentally and physically beat—empty—done. I decided to stay at the station instead.

I called my wife to check in and let her know I wasn't coming home. She had been very tense waiting for my call, knowing I was right in the middle of the mess she was watching on the news. She knew the rioters were attacking any law enforcement on the street and fire fighters as well. I reassured her that I was okay, needed to get some sleep, and would call her in the afternoon.

I changed out of my uniform and looked for a spot to sleep on the floor of the station gym, near the supervisor's locker room. The whole station was busier than usual and at that point lying down anywhere looked pretty damn good. As the third day of the riots wore on, I came to regret that decision.

Constant foot traffic, slamming doors, shouts, commands, and heavy boots, from regular station personnel all made getting to sleep difficult. National Guardsman were also arriving, using the restrooms and shower facilities, or trying to catch some shut eye on the floor as I was doing. In the long run, however, it was still a better alternative than trying to stay awake for the 90-minute ride home, driving over the lane dividing road dots on the freeway, half-asleep. Unfortunately, it was not exactly restorative sleep.

Friday, May 1st

The LAPD was being held accountable by everyday citizens, officials, and especially the media for their bad decision-making in the first hours of the riots. It's important to keep in mind that those LAPD officers were just following orders. Still, the decisions made and not made by their superior officers darkened the reputation of the entire department.

They were law enforcement officers, just like all of us, but they were human beings as well. Many had never witnessed the type of violence and ruthless behavior they were exposed to during the riots. They were as astonished at the ferocity of the rioters as were the public who were looking to them for protection.

A young undercover LAPD officer, Martha Defoe told of a chilling experience she has never forgotten.

"All of it was pretty intense, I mean you see your city up in smoke. But I will have to say ... this is one that's always stuck with me. I do remember having to stand with a Korean-American family, having to pull the remains of their family members (out of a charred building) that they had actually stayed inside trying to protect, basically, their livelihood.

People who had nothing to do with them whatsoever, they were paying the price for it. Their businesses, their homes, their family members being killed--burnt. Having to watch charred bodies come out of these businesses basically reduced to ashes."

As it did many other police officers, Defoe spoke of how the riots had marked her thinking.

"I just felt a lot of hate. I've never thought that the riots were like a race war. I just have a lot of hate. I've always had a lot of black friends—some of my best friends. But every time I looked at a black person, someone from the African-American community, I felt a lot of anger. [It seemed] they felt it was an opportunity for them to commit crimes ... to loot and hurt people, and all for what?

So for a long time I felt hate and it wasn't until the news media were talking about the people who were attacked at Florence and Normandie— one was a male white and one was a male Hispanic; who were just about killed, but they're alive today because of black residents who saw this on TV and they ran to that intersection and they helped these people. For me that was huge and it helped me get over it."

～

Early Friday morning, reports of snipers firing on LAPD officers, the expansion of the dusk-to-dawn curfew, the prohibition of the sale of ammunition, and the sale of gasoline for vehicles only, dominated the morning news.

At the outset of the third day of rioting, the military was officially engaged. After consulting with Governor Wilson and Mayor Bradley, President George H.W. Bush ordered 3,000 to 4,000 federal troops and 1,000 riot-trained federal law enforcement officers to Los Angeles.

Friday afternoon, officials in Washington D.C. and Los Angeles announced that a federal grand jury had been convened. The Justice Department was likely to seek criminal indictments of the four officers involved in the King beating. This decision would later result in two of the four officers acquitted in the King trials, Officer Laurence Powell and Sgt. Stacy Koon, being retried and convicted on federal charges of violating King's civil rights, specifically classified as willfully using and permitting unreasonable force. Officers Timothy Wind and Theodore Briseno were acquitted on federal charges. King would later be awarded $3.8 million by the city of Los Angeles.

Moments after the announcement of the convening of the federal grand jury and the Justice Department action, Rodney G. King, the man whose videotaped beating created a national furor over police brutality, broke his long silence to speak about the violence that had been inflicted in his name.

In a brief emotional televised statement, on the third day of the riots, he said these simple words: "People ... can we just get along?"

Later Friday evening, additional federal troops and National Guardsman were deployed into the Los Angeles area. President Bush addressed the nation regarding the violence in Los Angeles, denouncing "random terror and lawlessness" and announced that he would place 6,000 National Guard members under federal control.

The dawn-to-dust curfews took a heavy toll on area merchants that were still able to stay open. They suffered significant losses in sales, despite cleanup efforts starting to begin in some of the heavily affected areas. By late Friday evening, the toll was close to 40 deaths, and more than 1,400 injuries with over 150 critically injured. Over 4,300 arrests were made and more than 4,500 fires set, with damage estimates to be over $500 million dollars. At least 3,100 businesses had been affected by rioting or looting, and it wasn't over yet.

How far would things go? During the riots, most people were stunned and afraid of what was going to happen next. Before things calmed down, there would be five days of extreme violence. Even after the riots subsided, sporadic attacks on people and property continued.

Everyone was trying to make sense of the riots. For days and weeks afterward, there were scores of interviews with survivors and eye witnesses. The citizens of Los Angeles had watched the events play out on television, but what they saw in the destruction were nameless faceless people committing crimes and being victimized. America wanted a closer look and the personal interviews provided it. Twenty years later, in 2012, memories of those who experienced the riots first hand were still fresh.

"The city was ablaze," remembered Cornelius Pettis, a businessman from the Florence and Normandie area. "The 911 line was busy. Fire trucks were being dispatched to other locations. We had to do the next best thing which was put the fire out [ourselves], and so we did the best we could to put the fire out."

~

The intensity of the disturbances began to dissipate over the next three nights—Friday-Sunday. I was mostly tied to inside watch commander and administrative duties, and scheduling issues. Early Saturday morning, May 2, 1992, the first of 6,000 alleged looters and arsonists were scheduled to begin appearing in court.

On that same day, approximately 30,000 people marched for racial healing. They marched in support of beleaguered merchants in Koreatown. The citywide curfew remained in place.

President Bush declared Los Angeles a disaster area and Mayor Bradley, named former Olympics organizer Peter V. Ueberroth to serve as the unpaid "czar" for the Rebuild L.A. effort. Throughout the day legions of volunteers armed with grit, gumption and cleaning supplies hit the streets of Los Angeles. The effort attracted residents from all races and all segments of the city and county. Citizens pitched in to help hand out food and shuttle residents without bus service.

Approximately 3,500 National Guard troops remained on the streets and in staging areas. For the first time since the violence erupted on Wednesday, there were no new reports of major fires or any significant riot-related criminal incidents.

Calm was restored slowly and I was able to get home to see my wife and son.

Sunday, May 3rd

The Rapid Transit District (RTD) resumed limited bus service into South Central Los Angeles during the day on Sunday. The Reverend Jesse Jackson met with leaders in Koreatown to urge an end to animosity between African-American and Korean-American communities. Los Angeles County Sheriff Sherman Block called for federal prosecution of those who targeted Korean-American merchants and for those who beat the white truck driver, Reginald Denny, during the unrest.

Later in the day federal authorities announced that the Federal Bureau of Investigation (FBI) and the U.S. Attorney General's office would investigate the torching of Korean-owned businesses and the attack on Denny. The Los Angeles County Jail population was busting at the seams with approximately 25,000 inmates.

Many school districts and colleges announced they would reopen on Monday.

Monday, May 4th

Although a new week had begun, Los Angeles was still reeling from the devastation that had shaken the city. Mayor Bradley announced the lifting of the dusk-to-dawn curfew, stating that he expected inquiries into the LAPD and National Guard delays in their responses to the crisis. Later in the evening, National Guard members shot and killed a motorist who allegedly tried to run them down, resulting in the first use of deadly force by the National Guard since their deployment on Thursday. Police, acting on tips, recovered truckloads of stolen merchandise, and federal, state, and local emergency officials announced that one-stop disaster assistance centers would be opening soon.

Democratic presidential hopeful Bill Clinton arrived in Los Angeles to meet with community leaders and to inspect hard-hit areas. Despite mounting criticism, LAPD Chief Gates defended his conduct in planning and responding to the disturbance, particularly in its early stages. Life was slowly stabilizing.

DEFINING MOMENTS

I left the station to go home shortly after midnight Sunday night, technically Monday morning. I was thoroughly exhausted after five grueling days and nights. As I reached the middle of the rear parking lot of the station, I saw a large group of male and female deputies huddled between several parked cars. They were up against an adjoining block wall the station shared with the Jet Strip, an adjacent strip joint.

Before reaching my car someone from the group yelled out for me to join them. They were having a beer together and relaxing after days of being strung tight. I walked over to them and said, "No, thanks. I'm exhausted."

Several of them came closer. One male deputy, a leader among his peers at the station, called out to me saying that he spoke for everyone.

"We are fully aware of what you tried to do on Wednesday afternoon. We all respect you and appreciated your leadership and decision making, especially during the initial moments of the riots at Florence and Normandie."

The deputy's words made me feel good in my exhaustion, even validated. I smiled. The words touched me emotionally.

"We want you to know that every one of us would have fully supported the operation and your decision had you been able to pull it off."

They held their beers high and cheered. More than one said they were honored that I had the confidence in them to pull off such a bold tactical plan under those conditions. I could see the toll the stress of the last five days had taken on them. I felt it too.

I paused for a moment considering my words. "As your supervisor I was extremely proud of how you all responded and handled yourselves, especially in light of the fact you were all very disappointed, as I was, in not being able to engage. Every one of you wanted to save lives and do the jobs we were trained and expected to do."

They toasted me, and as I walked to my car, someone called my name. I turned to wave back at them.

In unison, several of them stood at attention and saluted me. I returned their salute. Tears came to my eyes as I slipped into the driver's seat of my car under the cover of darkness.

I drove home silently, lost in thought and listening to music to unwind: "Love Song" by the Cure, "Wicked Game" by Chris Isaac, "Separate Ways" by Journey, and "Jeopardy" by the Greg Kahn Band. Flash-frame after flash-frame of last five days played over and over in my mind. The senselessness of the riots wouldn't leave my thoughts. Visions of the death and destruction, of engulfing flames, as buildings and businesses burned to the ground, consumed me. Worst of all was the impact of the chaos and fear etched into the faces of so many. Some lost their innocence and sense of security, while others would carry a feeling of helplessness. Most would never forget.

The next few weeks were a time of rebuilding—of souls, relations, and lives. Many lives changed forever, as thousands of people lost their jobs at businesses which had been destroyed, either on a temporary or permanent basis. Most of these people were not likely to receive new opportunities for benefits, retraining, or access to other jobs. In less than a week, the course of their lives had shifted direction—unexpectedly, undeniably and unforgivingly.

City leaders and law enforcement officials debated on how the rioting was handled by law enforcement and how to repair the damage. In hindsight, many continued to criticize the LAPD's lack of response to the initial stages of the disturbance. The patrol units continued to deal with tense emotions and animosity from the public over the next several weeks, even as economic recovery and rebuilding efforts were initiated by politicians and business leaders.

Calls for gang retribution toward police and sniper fire were common during this initial time period. Ramifications of the unrest were far-reaching as the aftershock of the verdicts stirred demonstrations, looting, and violence in such cities as San Francisco, Las Vegas, Atlanta, Tampa, Seattle, Toronto, Canada, and Washington D.C.

In San Francisco, police responded with a decisive show of force and squashed demonstrators after a night of massive looting. Issuing warnings, they herded the predominantly youthful crowd into a circle. They surrounded them, placing plastic handcuffs on them and carted them off to jail in buses.

Wednesday, May 13th

A large and unruly gathering of over 300 gang members staged a Unity Meeting at Jesse Owens Park in South Central Los Angeles. Although this park was just outside LASD jurisdiction, one of the field sergeants, Matt Towner, monitored the gathering for quite some time. The group later dispersed from the park and regrouped at the intersection of

107th Street and Budlong Avenue, inside LASD jurisdiction. Almost immediately, Lennox Station began receiving complaints from citizens in the neighborhood. Sergeant Towner continued to monitor the gang gathering, assessing the possibility of major trouble developing.

At the beginning of our PM shift, Sergeant McKenzie and I discussed our station's possible response before this large gathering moved to a location inside our jurisdiction. We began to organize and disperse tactical response equipment that would be needed in the event of a station mobilization. Due to the volatile post-riot atmosphere of the past few weeks, we recognized the need to be prepared.

While Sergeant Towner and several assisting units attempted to disperse the gang gathering in a low key manner, their vehicles were pelted with objects by the unruly crowd. We contacted Sergeant Towner and after having him leave the area, we quickly developed a tactical operations plan. A location for a command post was established. We determined what resources, both inside and outside of our department, we would need to handle the mounting threat.

Within 90 minutes we had set up the command post at the Department of Probation and Social Services (DPSS) building on Imperial Avenue. Two full platoons, consisting of 64 deputies per platoon, arrived. Those reinforcements included a special weapons team, an air unit, 250 National Guard troops, 30 California Highway Patrol officers, and representatives of several other police agencies. News reporters and their vans also arrived on scene at the command post looking for action to report.

The show of force we hit the street with was the turning point that allowed us to disperse the large gathering without incident or injury. The potential disturbance dispersed and moved back into LAPD's area.

An ironic twist to end this story was that Sergeant Towner, Sergeant McKenzie, and myself, later received formal written commendations signed by Captain Monroe. We were recognized for our leadership and organizational skills during this extremely successful operation that started outside of our jurisdictional boundary. This action was taken by the same captain, who just 15 days earlier shut down my plan and refused to engage the unruly and violent crowd at Florence and Normandie Avenues, only one short mile outside of our jurisdictional boundary.

Chapter 10
SHERIFF BLOCK'S VISIT

Sunday, May 17th

On this warm Sunday afternoon, I was assigned as the field sergeant to work the PM shift. More than 2 weeks had passed since the onset of events that changed our country. Cleanup was underway in earnest, and serious discussions were taking place within the South Central community.

I addressed the 3 PM briefing, covering the updated crime reports and intelligence information regarding the current state of the community. A few minutes into the briefing, and to the surprise of all, Sheriff Sherman Block walked into the briefing room. He sat down at the table, looked around and greeted everyone. His personal driver stood outside the door. After a few tense moments under the eye of the big boss, I finished the briefing and asked Sheriff Block if he had anything for us.

He stated that he was pleased with our station's overall performance during the riots and the days since. He diplomatically hinted that he had hoped the LAPD would have handled the situation differently from the outset.

A question burned on my lips. I wanted to ask, if I had ordered and deployed my 15-man emergency response team to Florence and Normandie during the initial moments of the riot, would he have backed me up. My heart pounded fiercely remembering those crucial moments with the captain in the watch commander's office telling me not to engage.

I had wondered what Sheriff Block would say if I ever had the opportunity to ask him what he thought of my plan. There he was and now I had my chance.

I stopped myself. This was not the right time to ask him a political and sensitive question in front of the deputies. My heart sank, thinking the opportunity might never come again. Still, I didn't want to upset him or put him in a bad spot. That wouldn't be good for either of us.

We completed the briefing and adjourned. Moments later I saw Sheriff Block leaving with his deputy driver. As I stood looking out the rear door of the station, he suddenly turned and walked past the briefing room toward me. Here was my chance to talk to him. I could stop him there in the hallway without a crowd. We made eye contact and he stopped in front of me.

He said, "Sergeant Weiss that was a very comprehensive briefing. Sounds like you have your guys ready and well prepared."

"Thank you, Sheriff. Would you mind if I ask you a very difficult and political question?"

He said, "No, son, go ahead."

As we stood alone face-to-face in the hallway, I told Sheriff Block I was the acting watch commander on the initial night of the riots. I outlined the extra personnel I had assembled as a mobile response team, along with my normal deployment numbers we had that night. I summarized my plan, acknowledging that I knew it was risky. I reminded him we were all watching Denny being beaten via the Channel 13 news helicopter. I told him the pressure I was under, with calls from the community pleading for help. I told him at that exact moment I was ready to activate the response team when Captain Monroe walked into my office and shut me down. I said I had begrudgingly followed his orders, but I did not swallow it well. I told him the missed opportunity was still bothering me.

We stood alone, in the hallway. Sheriff Block paused and wiped what looked like a tear from his cheek, and said directly. "I would have definitely supported your decision to go in, Sergeant."

I felt vindicated. I felt strong and on solid ground about my decision making. Sheriff Block's unequivocal response assured me I was thinking correctly, both tactically and rationally.

"I would have sent Lennox and Firestone Stations into the flash point had I known LAPD was never going to deploy." Sheriff Block again paused and said, "You would have been my hero for doing that."

He then turned around and walked a few steps away and turned to me one last time and said, "What a decision and gutsy call that would have been. We could have changed the course of history. Never again should this happen."

Chapter 11

A MERCHANT'S TALE

Young Chul, not his real name, was a Korean business owner in the Florence District of South Los Angeles from 1988-1992. After he was laid off from his accounting job with a clothing manufacturer, he decided to venture out and operate his own business. At the age of 37 he purchased and operated the Express Market, not its true name. This was a small convenience store that was approximately 675 square feet in size, in the area of Holmes Avenue and 67th Street, a rough area filled with gang shootings and controlled by the Florencia 13 gang. This area was patrolled by the Los Angeles County Sheriff's Firestone Station and was just a few blocks from the Los Angeles City limits.

Young described the first year of ownership as a touchy, tense, and frightening time as he would be the frequent victim of petty thefts and beer runs from his store. As time progressed he learned that generally only locals were his customers. Instead of chasing and confronting the petty theft suspects, who were mostly cholos (young Hispanic males often associated with street gangs), with violence or physical resistance, he was gradually able to negotiate with them on their return visits.

A video camera was set up inside the market. The building had no windows or back door, and consisted of only one large steel front door. He indicated to the thieves that he had their crime recorded on video camera, but no one knew it was not operational. The gang members respected the fact that he did not turn them into law enforcement and report the crimes or share the videos with law enforcement. As time passed they actually apologized to him as he worked with them by allowing them to take items from the store and developed a pay and owe system. If they were low on cash they were allowed to take what they needed, but agreed to cash their welfare check and other sources of aid when they received the checks, which was usually every two weeks. Without fail they returned and made good on their promises by cashing their checks at the store and paying off their loan they had made with him.

After a period of 1-2 years he rarely had any more problems of petty thefts. The occasional petty thefts were committed by young cholos who were out to prove themselves and had no fear, believing they were invincible. Young would contact the shot caller of the gang and point out who was stealing from him. This would usually result in the young cholo returning to apologize and indicating that he did not know Young was like one of them.

When the back of his store received graffiti one day he was able to bring the problem to the attention of the leadership of the gang. They recruited several artists from within their ranks to paint a beautiful mural of the Lady of Guadalupe over the graffiti. Young never had any graffiti issues again.

Young's market was considered by the gang as their family market now and was off limits to graffiti, theft, robbery, and burglary, as he was considered a friend.

As time went on Young would purchase gifts for his neighborhood customers during Quinceanera celebrations—a significant rite of passage in the Hispanic culture for 15-year old girls as they transition from childhood to womanhood—and they in return showed their respect for him by also providing a gift for him or a family member during a major milestone. As the relationship and mutual trust evolved some of the cholos would remove their sawed-off shotguns and other weapons from their rear waistband after entering his market. They would place the weapons behind the counter when they were shopping in his market as a sign of respect.

Instead of hiring Korean helpers at his store, Young hired people from the neighborhood; one Hispanic and another Guatemalan man. It also helped that Young, who had taken adult and college classes after entering the country at a young age, could converse in spanish as well as in english and korean. This allowed him to communicate effectively with his customers and not be misunderstood. He also set up two pinball machines for the kids at the front of the store, which provided some form of entertainment for the neighborhood kids. Young had developed a rapport and trust that would never be broken. It was to pay off.

As the other local businessmen who owned other stores and businesses nearby flaunted their alleged wealth by driving Mercedes Benz's and dressing well off, Young wore the same worn jacket and never displayed any signs of being affluent. Although the gang members shopped at various other businesses due to necessity, Young was the most respected and frequented of all of them. They would routinely call him "boss" as another sign of respect. He gave to the community, was humble, and acted as if he was one of them. While the owner of this market for four years, he was never a victim of an armed robbery or burglary. The other business owners would ask him how he did so much business for having such a small store and why he was never robbed or burglarized.

On the first day of the riot Young was working at his market. He had no anticipation or word that any problems were developing in the community during the Rodney King trial or on that particular day. As the riots initially erupted at Florence and Normandie Avenues, approximately 3½ miles from his market, nearby businesses soon suffered from some looting and vandalism. Young was scared and concerned. He stayed overnight locked inside his market for the next 12-15 hours. He put his heart and soul into the market and he felt like he wanted to die as he saw the mobs of people destroy and loot one store after another. After he had been laid off from his accounting job he decided to take out a loan and purchase the store. All he could think of was that his market was his whole life and he had to survive for the sake of his family, just like when he learned how to initially deal with the thefts and other issues when he first opened the market in 1988. He had no other options in his mind.

Outside of Young's market stood several of the Florencia 13 gang members armed and protecting the market from the Crips and Bloods gangs and other looters that infiltrated the area. Their presence and sheer numbers averted any damage to his building. The gang members, who stayed nearby even as the National Guard later arrived in the area, stood guard well past the sixth and last day of the riots and looting.

Young, who went home on the morning of the second day of the riots, returned to the market early on the third day of the riots and opened to a long line of local customers. His business and income tripled for weeks as he was the only business out of 13 nearby businesses to survive the looting, arson fires, and destruction. The community needed him as much as he needed them.

Young was never injured, threatened, or assaulted during the riots, even as he drove back and forth to home in the early morning or late evening hours. Although other business owners armed themselves, he never once was armed. Young also received some protection from the nearby Firestone Sheriff's Station, since he had contributed yearly to the Christmas fund and other activities for the station.

In July of 1992, two short months after the riots, Young sold his market. He was constantly working long hours and 7 days a week, which allowed for no family life or time for church and worshipping. He also wanted a larger and more professional type of business in a safer area that would be closer to home. Approximately 3 months later he opened a dry cleaner's in the Southern California area, which he still owns and operates today.

EPILOGUE

By the time it was over, the riot's flames, looting, and violence resulted in at least 53 deaths and over 2,300 physical injuries, of which at least 228 were classified as critical. Over 12,000 arrests were made and 7,000 fires blazed. Approximately 3,100 businesses were affected by looting and rioting with property damage estimated at nearly $1 billion. Once the turmoil subsided, news reports analyzed and officials addressed their opinions of the pre-riot climate as well as what occurred during and after.

On Wednesday, May 6, 1992, the Los Angeles Times reported that Sheriff Block was watching news reports on television as the violence erupted. He expected at any second that he would see police arrive.

"Had I realized that officers would not take action, I would have sent sheriff's deputies from the Firestone Station to intervene. It's my belief a show of force at that location and at that time might not have stopped everything, but certainly would have had a significant impact."

The Sheriff was amazed to read after the riots had abated, that there were 20 LAPD officers just a block away from Florence and Normandie Avenues when the rioting started. "That doesn't make any sense at all," he said.

Sheriff Block said that he believes LAPD officers "gave an aura of legitimacy" to the looting when they stood by without taking action, an image that was captured in many televised news reports.

On Thursday May 7, 1992, the Los Angeles Times reported Sheriff Block said the Sheriff's Department had updated its own contingency plans for civil disorder just three weeks prior to the riots. He indicated the Department's field operations staff assembled a 9½ page contingency plan two weeks before the King verdicts. The plan was called Operation Monarch, a play on the last name of LAPD beating victim Rodney G. King. Sheriff Block declined to discuss the specific contents of the plan, but indicated that a similar contingency plan would have been crucial to the LAPD's efforts to maintain order.

After Sheriff Block's statements, the Los Angeles County Board of Supervisors voted to establish the Webster Commission. This commission later submitted a detailed analysis of the crisis, called The Webster Report: The City of Crisis, a 222-page report, spearheaded by former FBI and Central Intelligence Agency Director William H. Webster to investigate the response of law enforcement and the National Guard to the riot. One of the report's findings, discussed in the Los Angeles Times on October 21, 1992, indicated the LAPD should have sought assistance from the LASD and other agencies.

Another finding of the commission as indicated in the Daily News on October 22, 1992, was that LAPD's leadership deficiencies appear to have resulted in a failure to mobilize and deploy quickly, and the possibility that an opportunity to contain the disorder may have been lost at the outset. Also, the Los Angeles County Board of Supervisors asked the Los Angeles County Grand Jury to investigate the police agencies' slow response at the outset of the riots.

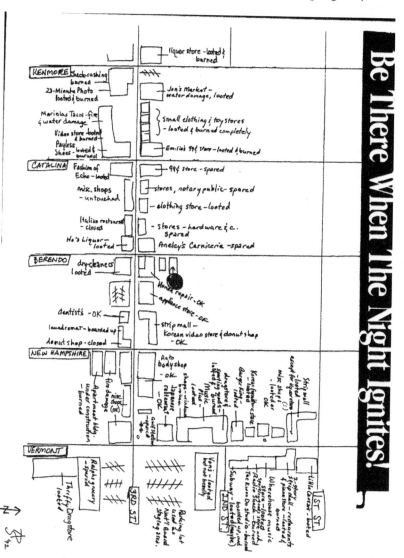

Map courtesy of Alan P. Scott

Hand drawn map made by Alan P. Scott for his relatives from back east, which depicts the damage done to his surrounding neighborhood during the 1992 Los Angeles riots.

AUTHOR'S NOTE

The Los Angeles Riots of 1992, and the more recent civil disturbances on August 9, 2014, in Ferguson, Missouri, and on April 18, 2015, in Baltimore, Maryland, were similar regarding the manner in which law enforcement responded to the initial stages of these civil disturbances. Whether it was the police beating of Rodney King in Los Angeles, the police shooting of Michael Brown in Ferguson, or the in custody injuries and death of Freddie Gray in Baltimore, law enforcement did not respond properly to the disturbances resulting from these incidents.

Law enforcement has the duty, responsibility, and obligation to protect. The lack of an immediate, effective and coordinated response to these disturbances led to needless deaths, injuries, and destruction. Ironically, countless citizens and groups voiced concern and frustration with police officers failing to engage with rioters and allowing looting and destruction to occur. Police were better prepared and trained than they demonstrated in each of these incidents. These difficult lessons learned should never again be repeated.

Public pressure, concern with image over safety, and the issue of political correctness should never again interfere with law enforcement performing its functions. Passive response to these initial disturbances allowed disorder to develop into major riots. Treating people with respect and allowing them to vent their frustrations is one thing, but standing by and allowing people to kill, assault, rob, steal, and destroy property should never be acceptable.

ABOUT THE AUTHOR

Bill Weiss was a fairly new patrol sergeant with the Los Angeles County Sheriff's Department in April of 1992, and was promoted only 20 months earlier to that rank. He was the acting watch commander of a patrol station, a position customarily held normally by a tenured lieutenant, during the initial hours of the most violent and destructive civil disturbance in the United States in the last century.

Never Again is a true account of this never-before-told insight into the hours leading up to, during, and after the Los Angeles Riots erupted on April 29, 1992. The story reveals the emergent preparations and tough decisions Weiss faced while preparing Lennox Sheriff's Station in South Los Angeles to handle this unbelievable event.

Drawing upon his training and experience, Weiss reveals the sequence of events behind the scenes as another nearby major law enforcement agency is thrust into the limelight, finding itself totally unprepared to deal with this deadly and rapidly evolving crisis.

Never Again shows, detail by detail, how close Weiss was to potentially changing the course of history. In those initial hours of turmoil, Weiss struggled against his trained self-discipline of a law enforcement official following orders and with an instinctual drive to take action. In the moment of crisis, he must deal with a commanding officer in opposition to his daring plan of action. To this day, he feels a surge of regret at the recollection of these events. A moment that could have changed the outcomes that rocked Los Angeles was lost. Viewing newspaper articles and photos, hearing personal stories and media reports, he still struggles to come to terms with what could have been.

A 32-year veteran of the Los Angeles County Sheriff's Department, Bill Weiss worked various patrol, custody, administrative, investigative, and special assignments during his outstanding career. He had a reputation for having an uncanny ability to apprehend fleeing suspects and tracking down local serial burglars and street robbers. Either as a deputy, sergeant, or lieutenant, he was viewed as an aggressive, yet diverse, fair, honest, and hard-working cop who spent the majority of his law enforcement career in a supervisory and leadership capacity.

Weiss was an incident commander for several major tactical incidents throughout the years. He is a graduate of the University of Southern California, with a Master's degree in Public Administration. Weiss is a contributing author in a section titled, A Lingering Guilt, in the recently published book, Writer to Writer. Since retiring as a lieutenant in January of 2013, he continues to reside in California.

HISTORICAL REFERENCE

El Palacio Apartments, La Cienega Blvd., and more.
La Cienega Boulevard is a major road that runs north and south between Hawthorne on the south side and the famed Sunset Strip/ Sunset Boulevard in West Hollywood. One of Hollywood's major thoroughfares, it was built to freeway standards in the late 1940s as part of State Route 170. The SR 170 freeway was never completed south of U.S. Route 101. What makes La Cienega unique is the stretch from just north of Fairview Blvd in Inglewood to Rodeo Road in Los Angeles. It's a divided, limited access highway with few traffic signals. Emergency call boxes such as can be found along freeways were also installed along that stretch in the 1970s.

Fountain Avenue, six miles long, runs parallel between Sunset Boulevard to the north and Santa Monica Boulevard to the south. It runs from Silver Lake west to La Cienega Blvd. There are not many businesses on Fountain Avenue, but there are some notable buildings.

For example, not too far from the northeast corner of La Cienega Boulevard and Fountain Avenue, is the El Palacio, an apartment building, with Spanish arches. Beautifully landscaped, it's a perfect example of early Hollywood. The African-American movie star, Dorothy Dandridge, nominated for an Oscar in 1954 for work in the movie, Carmen Jones, lived and after committing suicide, died there.

Many Hollywood celebrities came to sad ends, as they still do today. A few miles away is Pierce Brothers Westwood Village Memorial Park and Mortuary. Marilyn Monroe, who also spent time at the El Palacio, is buried there, as is the grave of Natalie Wood, an actress who drowned off Catalina Island in 1981 after apparently stumbling off the yacht she owned with husband Robert Wagner. Playboy playmate Dorothy Stratten, killed in 1980 by a jealous husband, shares the same final resting place.

~

Reginald Denny Update

Lucky to be alive, today Denny suffers from nerve damage in his eyes, hearing loss, and has suffered severe financial setbacks because of the ordeal, but in interviews has implied he doesn't allow the incident to hold him back. In an interview on the Phil Donahue show Denny said, "What people seem to forget is that it was black folks that saved my life … on one hand some tried to kill me or do me in. On the other hand, some tried to save me because I'm not the enemy."

He continued, "What did it do, them thinking it was going to change their situation? It didn't do anything but get them in more trouble."

Rescuer Bennie Newton

Sadly, almost a year later to the day after he saved Fidel Lopez's life, Reverend Bennie Newton lost his battle with Leukemia. He died a hero, on April 24, 1993, and not only for his instant heroism attained during the King riots. He was an ex-con who believed in love among the races.

After serving time in such prisons as San Quentin for armed robbery, drug possession and pimping, Benny Newton went into business for himself, launching a carpet cleaning business and hiring ex-cons. For some that was the second chance they may never have gotten were it not for Newton.

From there he founded the Light of Love Outreach Ministry in Westchester, where he ministered to young people in county jails and on Skid Row. He was on his way to a peace rally when he heard of the beatings on Florence and Normandie.

During Lopez's recovery, Newton gave $3,015 in donations he had received after the riots to help Lopez. In the months before his death, the two men became good friends. Lopez had made several trips to Newton's bedside during the last few weeks of his life. The same racial issues that tore Los Angeles apart brought two men from different backgrounds together.

Cornelius Pettus Account

At one point a fire hydrant was opened. The news cameras filmed people gathering water with buckets. When asked about it. Mr. Pettus said he wasn't sure how that happened or who did it. But he and others made use of the serendipitous event.

"We used that water to go into Ace Glass to protect their property because we were right next door and knew we would be next to burn. I have no idea who set the fire.

Everybody was running. There was a liquor store across the street that started on fire. There was fire after fire....

I was able to protect my business since I had worked for the Gas Company. I knew how to shut off the gas at Ace Glass so there wouldn't be an explosion. Then we used the water from the fire hydrant filled buckets and put the fire out.

We prevented looters from coming into our shop by staying there for three days. The looters only went into places where owners were absent.

I hope there will never be a riot like this again. So many people were hurt. Families were hurt and lost businesses. Some have still not recovered 20 years later."

Many wonder what caused the riots. Among the people of South Central there were layers of reasons tension ran so high.

"There was a feeling of hopelessness," Pettus explained. "People were not satisfied with the verdict and they chose to take action in that way."

The loss was astronomical. "Even after some businesses were rebuilt structurally, the city would not allow them to return with their liquor licenses."

For years community activists had been under pressure to rid the community of what was determined to be a vast number of liquor stores in the area. Community leaders, residents and elected officials blamed the concentration of liquor stores in South-Central Los Angeles for contributing to crime, blight and alcoholism in their neighborhoods. As destructive as the riots were, they provided convenient reasoning to disallow the renewal of 100s of liquor licenses and reopening of stores. The battle continued and on January 19, 1995, the Los Angeles City Council directed planning officials to make full use of new state laws that helped municipalities slow the spread of inner-city liquor stores.

Pettus described what happened to these businesses as a result of the riots. "Some [store owners] had paid $250,000 and were hurting after the riots. They went out of business because they couldn't make it just selling dry groceries in the area. A lot of businesses were lost. Many owners lost everything—their life's savings. They lost their merchandise and often a place to live because if they weren't generating income, they lost their homes behind it."

The ripple effect of a riot or any other devastating event is often felt for years and sometimes decades later. Even after the clean-up began in the impacted areas, it was difficult for many to pick up the pieces and put their lives back together. Some never did.

Also, what of the apparent LAPD abandonment during the initial stages of the violence? How did the business owners perceive it from their end?

Pettus was less judgmental than other business owners. "I'm sure they were caught off guard. The media interviews had them down at 54th and Van Ness which was the metro bus station and they were under instructions not to leave the area. A lot of the officers were saying, they needed to be on the streets, but their commanding officer said, 'No you're not going to the streets'."

As was perceived by many, the media played a part in escalating the violence. Television announcements that described a free-for-all, with no fear of retribution were perceived as if to say, "Come and Get it!"

"The media really hurt a lot of business owners," noted Pettus, "because we kept hearing on the news—on national television—that there were no police at Florence and Normandie. So the looters came.

It was very destructive, what the media did as far as announcing alarms are not being answered, police are not responding, and it really snowballed from that point.

The LAPD had the ability to handle it and from the interviews following the riots, it appeared they wanted to be on the streets but they were instructed not to leave the metro station on 54th and Van Ness. Had they been allowed to do their jobs, a lot of property would have been saved and lives would have been salvaged."

The interviewer turned the conversation toward what seemed to be the most targeted group during the riots, Korean-American business people. Why did they bear the brunt of such irreversible destruction?

Pettus paused thoughtfully and after taking a breath offered his response. "Once you take a man's business, you take away his home and a way for him to provide for his family.

I don't think Korean Americans were targeted so much, I think it was because they were local businesses. I was in an area where most of the grocery markets were owned by Korean Americans.

There were furniture stores and all types of businesses being vandalized because of the irresponsible media. It was total chaos."

Pettus says that in some ways things have gotten better, but there are still vacant lots 20 years later. "I'm sure a lot of people are afraid to go back into business in those areas. A lot of them have probably relocated or gone into business doing something else. There is a lot that has not been rebuilt in 20 years and that's really a tragedy."

Yes, it is.

~

South Central LA is infamous gang territory, although some gangs have contingents in other parts of the country. Excluding those who live in gang territory and have a good understanding of gang culture, most of what people understand is what is presented by the media and motion picture industry. The following is a brief history.

Prominent Los Angeles Gangs

Gang activity in South Central Los Angeles finds its inception with the post-World War II economic decline that led to joblessness and poverty. Although many black and Latino Americans fought side by side with whites in World Wars I and II, racial segregation continued into the 50s and 60s, leading to the formation of black street clubs. As Black Nationalist organizations such as the Black Panther Party and the Black Power Movement waned, young African-American men who were excluded from the Boy Scouts and other youth organizations pulled together and formed extended families, eventually becoming what we define today as gangs.

Although Florencia 13 held a presence, probably the most famous gangs are notorious rivals, the Crips and Bloods. Ironically, the year before the King riots they had agreed to a truce. They had reportedly done so to unify against police. The two largest L.A. street gangs, the Crips and the Bloods, began working together to make political demands of the police and the L.A. political establishment. The following is a background on three of the major gangs who made Los Angeles home.

Florencia 13

Most of South Central was known for its African-American gangs, but there are also Hispanic gangs scattered among them. The influx of Mexican immigrants before World War II came as a result of hiring by the railroad. They were hired to lay track between Los Angeles and Long Beach, and many settled in South Central. By the 60s, Florencia 13 (F13) was well established in the area. The gang got its name from the major street, Florence Avenue, intersecting with Normandie as the nucleus of the 1992 riots. Although they were always outnumbered by rival black gangs, they earned a reputation for fierceness.

The Crips

The Crips, who are comprised primarily of African-American members, were founded in Los Angeles in 1969. The growth and power of the gang took off in the early 1980s when crack cocaine hit the streets, and by the late 80s the Crips were one of the largest street gangs in the county. By 1978, there were 45 Crips gangs, called sets, operating in Los Angeles. The Crips are said to be one of the largest and most violent associations of street gangs in the United States, with an estimated 30,000 to 35,000 members at the time of this writing. The members identify themselves by wearing blue, although the practice has become less so due to police crackdowns on gang members.

The Bloods

Also getting a start in Los Angeles, the Bloods formed to compete against The Crips. Established in the 60s as The Piru street gang, the Bloods membership rose dramatically in the 80s with the distribution of crack cocaine and spread throughout the country. At the time, the Crips outnumbered Bloods three to one and in order to assert dominance, the Bloods became increasingly violent. Their rivalry with the Crips is well known.

Many people think gangs are a relatively recent phenomenon, but gangs have always existed. In the U.S., evidence suggests their emergence on the East Coast around 1783, around the time the American Revolution ended. These first gangs were more like clubs. The more serious street gangs likely did not emerge until the early part of the nineteenth century. Gangs formed as people who emigrated from foreign countries stuck together, aware that there was power in numbers.

In the early 30s and 40s, in Los Angeles and other parts of the country an old school Mexican American/Latino subculture called pachucos emerged. Many were part of street gangs and were associated with the Zoot Suit, nightlife and flamboyant behavior. The movie, Zoot Suit by Luis Valdez, gives a good characterization of their history.

A discussion of the Rodney King Riots in the early 1990s cannot be understood without looking back in history to two very significant events of similar nature. Did events that were set into motion half a century prior set the pace for the present day calamity?

Zoot Suit Riots

The worst mob violence in Los Angeles history took place in August of 1942.

A group of Mexican-American teens from LA's 38th Street were convicted of having murdered a young man by the name of Jose Diaz after a 10 minute fight in the area. They were sent to San Quentin.

The summer was hot, and 50,000 sailors went into the City of Los Angeles to let off steam. There were daily rumbles as the servicemen would fight with the Mexican-American youth, mostly because they didn't like the way the boys were dressed. Sailor Reno Sanetti said, "At the base, they told us to go down to the sail shop and they sewed 13 pennies into the neckerchief … so if any pachucos came after you, you could use that neckerchief as a billy club."

On June 3, 1943, the city exploded. A sailor and a zoot suit member had an altercation during the day and that evening the Zoot Suit Riots had begun. Sailors went into a movie theater using gun belts and chains as 12 and 13 year-old boys were beaten because of the clothes they wore.

The next night, 100s of sailors took the fight beyond downtown LA and into the heart of the barrio, seeking out Mexican-American youth who were staying away from downtown theaters and bars.

The sailors scoured the barrio for youth and then targeted any Mexican who crossed their path. Even though at the time, Mexicans were not the only ones wearing zoot suits, the zoot suit was given racial connotations. The Zoot Suit riot was generalized to include all Mexicans.

The kids from the barrio organized to fight back.

Rudy Leyvas, the brother of one of the boys arrested that past August recalls: "There was an alley behind this theater, and a lot right next to it and it was just jammed. We were waiting—it was already getting dark.

So about 20-30 guys came into the street so when the sailors got there we could see them. As soon as they got out there, here comes those truckloads—truckloads of sailors and civilians.

They let out a cry, 'There they are! There they are!'

They came in and once they came all the way in we all came out.

I myself had a bat and I used it. There were people hurt on both sides."

Rudy Leyvas also met a man on the street who gave him his car to use for the night saying, "Leave it anywhere on Central Avenue and I'll come and get it. All I want you to do is get one of those white guys for me."

Carlos Espinoza was there too. He talks of how the youth fought back:

"At night time [the sailors] came. We would just disappear. But we found out the best thing to do to get even with them was to watch them on Whittier Blvd. When there were four or five guys in a car, we'd follow them until they came to a stop and there would be another car in front of them, we'd run out and open one door and start pounding the hell out of them. Get the driver out and beat him up and start pounding the other guys."

It wasn't just male civilians who fought alongside the sailors. Teenaged girls and young women were just as committed.

[Female Civilian, 16 years old at the time]

"…we got my mother's car and went and picked up Marines. Los Angeles was like a war zone and we had to do something about it. The pachucos had just taken over. I felt that I was doing my share for the war effort."

News of the riots spread. Sailors from Northern California and as far away as Las Vegas arrived by the thousands in support of their fellow servicemen. On the fifth day of the riots, 5,000 civilians showed up to help the sailors.

The rest of the story sounds very familiar and reminiscent of the LA riots in 1992:

During about a week of rioting, the LAPD was nowhere to be found. They only appeared in riot ravaged-areas to arrest victims. According to one soldier, "The shore patrol would pick up the Mexican kids and throw them in jail and pick up the sailors and drop them off a couple blocks away and tell them to get back to their ships."

On June 8th, military authorities and civic leaders declared the city off limits to servicemen. The rioting ended. In the wake of the riots the governor appointed a citizen's committee to determine what had caused them.

A similar war was waged in 1965 and perhaps foreshadowed what was to come almost 30 years later.

The Watts Riots

The worst unrest Los Angeles saw since the Zoot Suit Riots and before the Rodney King riots broke out in the Watts district on August 11, 1965, after a black motorist was pulled over for drunk driving. Marquette Frye borrowed his mother's car and with his brother as passenger, left his house. Police pulled him over for driving recklessly. They weren't far from home so Marquette's brother ran home to alert his mother, Rena Price.

Mother and son quickly arrived at the scene to find Marquette being arrested for drunk driving. He had admitted it and was calmly going along with police.

A minor argument ensued with Rena Price and soon turned physical. Shortly thereafter, angry mobs formed and began shouting and throwing objects at police. After Frye, his brother and mother were arrested, a huge crowd formed in the area.

Under a barrage of rocks and concrete, police tried to break up the gathering, at first comprised mostly of neighborhood residents. To no avail, the crowd continued to swell.

The next day, black community leaders came together to encourage calm but their efforts failed. The National Guard, 4,000 strong, was called in for support.

What followed were six days of looting and arson, largely confined to white-owned stores and businesses that were said to have perpetuated resentment in the neighborhood due to perceived unfairness. Again, a familiar tone of the riots in 1992 was the following scenario.

White Americans were fearful of the breakdown of social order in Watts, especially since white motorists were being pulled over by rioters in nearby areas and assaulted.

The end result was 34 deaths and over $40 million in property damage. As would later be said about the Rodney King Riots, blame would initially fall on poverty and unemployment, although a later investigation implicated police racism.

Fueled by heated emotion, the Watts riots broke out just as quickly as did the Rodney King riots. It wasn't until six days later—again as in the King riots—the city of Los Angeles tried to pick up the pieces in its aftermath.

After visiting Watts post-riot, civil rights leader Dr. Martin Luther King had this to say, "What did Watts accomplish but the deaths of 34 Negros and injuring 1000s more? What did it profit the Negro to burn down the stores and factories in which he sought employment? The way of rights is not a way of progress but a blind alley of death and destruction which wreaks its havoc hardest among the rioters themselves."

Five months after the Watts riot, news anchor Howard K. Smith reported, "Watts has become the most analyzed community in America. Why did the riot take place? Was it a riot, or was it something else?" He goes on to introduce an important discussion—one that should be had after every uprising. "The common people of Watts or the men and women who took part in the riot or support the goals of the rioters claim that they have been ignored. Come to us they say, if you want the truth and come to us, looking for the truth."

In response to the fact that African Americans feel as though their needs are ignored, one Watts community member warned,

"You're going to create a black monster down here. And this monster is going to get larger and larger and pretty soon he's going to eat all of us up—even the Negros wearing neckties."

Is this what happened on Florence and Normandie in 1992? Did the monster called racial unrest, finally say, enough is enough?

One young man told Smith that when he was young he was pushed around by the white man, but no longer. He said "Negros are stepping up. They're waking up and they're going to do something about what the white man did to them in the past."

"What will the black man do?" Smith inquired.

"The black man will come up and take the white man's position and put him where the Negros are today."

Smith paused and then asked the man. "Is that why you rioted?"

"We rioted because the white man [is treating] the Negros unfairly. They're taking what they had—all the Negros had, just about. I've had enough of that."

"What are you going to do about it?"

The man responded matter-of-factly, "If necessary, start another riot … If I have to die for my rights, I will."

REFERENCES CITED

Reich, Kenneth. Chavez, Stephanie. "Block Says LAPD Response Made No Sense." Los Angeles Times. 6 May 1992: A1, A6.

Hubler, Shawn. Oliver, Myrna. Gordon, Larry. "Genesis of a Riot." Los Angeles Times. 7 May 1992: A9.

Serrano, Richard. Rohrlich, Ted. "Criticism Over Use of Force Inhibited Police, Gates Says." Los Angeles Times. 7 May 1992: A1, A8.

Serrano, Richard. "Redeploy Police, Riot Response Study Urges." Los Angeles Times. 21 October 1992: A1, A15.

McGreevy, Patrick. "Handling of Riots Assailed. Webster Report Criticizes Gates, Bradley, Council." Daily News. 22 October 1992: 1, 19.

Staff, Los Angeles Times. "Charting the Hours of Chaos." Los Angeles Times. 29 April 2002: B6, B7.

Woo, Elaine. Malnic, Eric. "Controversial LAPD Chief." Los Angeles Times. 17, April 2010: A1, A12, A13.

Fremon, Celeste. "Gang Violence, Daryl Gates & the Task of Making it Home on April 29, 1992." WitnessLA.com. 30, April 2012: 10, 11.

CPSIA information can be obtained at www.ICGtesting.com
Printed in the USA
BVOW08s1625091016

464567BV00003B/176/P